DO NOT REMOVE
CARDS FROM POCKET

ALLEN COUNTY PUBLIC LIBRARY

FORT WAYNE, INDIANA 46802

You may return this book to any agency, branch,
or bookmobile of the Allen County Public Library.

DEMCO

New Frontiers in Genetics

Sandy and Jerry Bornstein

Julian Messner  New York

Published by Julian Messner,
A Division of Simon & Schuster, Inc.
Simon & Schuster Building,
1230 Avenue of the Americas,
New York, New York 10020.
JULIAN MESSNER and colophon are trademarks of
Simon & Schuster, Inc.

Manufactured in the United States of America

Design by A Good Thing, Inc.

Library of Congress Cataloging in Publication Data

Bornstein, Sandy.
  New frontiers in genetics.

  Bibliography: p.
  Includes index.
  Summary: Discusses new advances in genetic science and
examines the benefits, risks, and potential problems
that these pose for the human community now and in the
future.
  1. Human genetics. 2. Human genetics—Social aspects.
3. Genetic engineering. 4. Genetic engineering—Social
aspects. [1. Genetics. 2. Genetic engineering]
I. Bornstein, Jerry. II. Title.
QH431.B63519 1984   573.2′1   83-23758
ISBN 0-671-45245-2

10 9 8 7 6 5 4 3 2 1

For Lisa and Danica
with Our Love

Other Books

by Sandy and Jerry Bornstein
  What Is Genetics?

by Jerry Bornstein
  Unions in Transition

Contents

Introduction

As a science genetics has come a very long way in a relatively short time. Not too long ago the science of heredity was just taking its first hesitating baby steps toward understanding inheritance and the genetic code. The theoretical and practical advances that have made genetics invaluable to medical science are very recent—just decades old.

In recent years the media has focused considerable attention on a new branch of genetics that is delving into the possibility of manipulating the genetic code. This field is called genetic engineering, and the very mention of that term triggers emotional and heated debate. Unfortunately much media coverage is distorted. On one extreme, it tends to sensationalize, conjuring up images of a Brave New World, of robotlike clones, and of monstrous new creatures. At the opposite extreme, the media coverage tends to bow uncritically before the god of scientific advancement. This view accepts optimistic speculation about the possible benefits of genetic engineering at face value and fails to probe into the possible dangers that lie ahead. In focusing so much attention on genetic engineering, the media obscures the tremendous developments and advances that have been made in others areas of genetics and takes the debate over genetic engineering out of context.

The goal of this book is to provide a framework for a balanced assessment of genetics today, including genetic engineering. We will of necessity review some basic points about the cell, the genetic program, the nature of DNA, which codes the genetic program, and cell division, but this book is not intended as an introduction to the science of genetics. For that the reader will have to turn elsewhere. Our primary task here is to describe the ways in which the knowledge of genetics that science has accumulated thus far is being used to serve the human community, including the benefits, risks, and potential problems posed for society's future.

We will discuss the ways in which medical scientists use genetic knowledge in the fight against birth defects, genetic disease, and cancer. We will describe the nature and types of genetic disease, what is known about their causes, and the mysteries that remain. We will survey the uses of genetics in analyzing the potential health hazards of pollutants. And finally we will discuss the issue of genetic engineering.

Genetics is a science that touches on the very basis of life on earth. The research and work being done today in this field will have a tremendous impact on the type of world we will live in tomorrow. The decisions being made today and in the years ahead will help shape the kind of society we become. Decisions on the uses of science and technology should not be left to the "experts," whether on the campus, in business, or in government. Society as a whole, and that includes you and us, has a right and an obligation to participate in these decisions.

It is our hope that this book will provide readers with a sound basis for understanding what genetics has done for society so far and what potential benefits it promises for the future. It can also offer a framework to help readers participate intelligently in the debates that are raging today and that will continue tomorrow on the appropriate uses of genetics and the future of society.

Sandy and Jerry Bornstein

1

Medicine
and
Genetics

The interest of medical science in genetics is quite recent. But this is not surprising because genetics is a relatively young field. The breakthroughs in appreciating the impact heredity has on the development and functioning of living organisms has only recently progressed beyond the vague recognition that parents in some manner pass on certain of their traits to their offspring. The elementary findings of Gregor Mendel, the father of genetics, who studied the inheritance of distinct traits controlled by single gene pairs in pea plants over a century ago, have given way to a far more sophisticated understanding of the complexities of the interaction between heredity and environment.

Genetics isn't simply the study of the inheritance of traits from our parents. Genetics also deals with how we live, grow, and develop. The way an individual develops is a result of the dynamic and complex interaction between the instructions coded in that person's genetic program and the environment in which that program is put into action. Our genetic program operates every moment of our lives. Our understanding that the development of life itself is the result of a complex and well-balanced interdependency between the genetic blueprint provided by the parents to the fertilized egg and the complex environment in which this genetic plan is put into action is a relatively recent development.

The process of developing this new knowledge of genetics and applying it to medical diagnosis and treatment has at the same time been conditioned by and been a cause of the scientists' continually increasing ability to go from the specific to the general and back to the specific, armed with greater understanding. To develop medical applications for genetics, you must be able to go from a theoretical understanding of heredity to an ability to pinpoint and understand how heredity works in specific situations. You must be able to understand the relationship between normal mechanisms of heredity and normal development, on the one hand, and the relationship between abnormalities in these mechanisms and genetic disease and birth defects, on the other hand. The more we know, the more we can do. The more we know about the specifics of genetic disease, the more accurate our diagnostic abilities can become, and the more effective our attempts at treatment can be.

Over the course of evolution, human beings have developed a genetic program that permits a wide variation in traits which are compatible with normal development and health—perhaps a greater degree of acceptable variation than many other species on earth. But there are limits to the variation that can be tolerated, and when those limits are transgressed, genetic disease occurs.

GENETIC DISEASE

It is now clear that in one form or another genetics plays a role in many diseases and disorders. Despite the unsolved mysteries of the exact mechanics of many genetic diseases, there is a clear relationship between genetic alterations and genetic disease or birth defects. The many disorders in which genetics, and not environment, is of paramount importance can be subdivided into three categories:

Single gene origin. This type of disorder is caused by an error in the genetic information stored by the genetic code at a single point. Depending on the nature of the gene product, the abnormality may be expressed either by the action of a single abnormal gene or by the concerted action of both members of the gene pair. Such an error can lead the organism to manufacture a defective gene product, perhaps a wrong protein or an ineffective enzyme. Although a great deal of variation can probably be tolerated, under certain circumstances, such an error can have quite far-reaching consequences. The production of an erroneous enzyme or protein may have multiple effects on the organism, but it is caused by a mistake in a single piece of genetic information.

Chromosome abnormalities. Missing, extra, or rearranged pieces of otherwise normal bits of genetic information cause chromosome disorders. Because large chunks of genetic material that cause a significant imbalance in the genetic program are involved, chromosomal abnormalities usually affect multiple aspects of development, and more than one organ system in the body. With this generalized disruption of genetic balance, mental development and the ability to thrive are seriously affected in most cases. In addition to this generalized abnormal development, specific symptoms related to the particular pieces of genetic information involved in the chromosomal abnormality are frequently seen. Perhaps half of all early spontaneous abortions, or miscarriages, result from chromosomal abnormalities so serious that it is impossible for the embryo to develop normally and survive until birth.

Multifactorial inheritance. Many human traits are influenced by the contributions and interaction of a number of minor genes, rather than by the action of a single major gene. Some traits are influenced by the combined interaction of as few as ten genes, others by the interaction of as many as two hundred genes. Height and intelligence are examples of the types of traits controlled by multifactorial inheritance. An abnormal alteration in any one of the interacting genes may have an impact on the incidence of genetic disease. Many congenital defects, such as cleft lip and cleft palate are attributed to such modes of inheritance as well.

There are essentially two different types of genetic disruption. The first type results from abnormalities on the molecular level. This type incorporates single gene and multifactorial genetic diseases. The second type involves abnormalities that entail distrubances in the discrete, separate chains of genetic material known as the chromosomes, which are found in the nucleus of almost every cell and are visible under the microscope. Let us take a look at these two types of genetic disruptions in more detail.

BIOCHEMICAL GENETICS

As long ago as 1909 a scientist named A.E. Garrod suggested that certain clinically observable diseases were caused by disturbances on the molecular level of the body's normal metabolism, or ability to process nutrients into needed cellular products. He postulated that these deficiencies could be inherited, and he therefore called them "inborn errors of metabolism."

Garrod studied a disease known as alkaptanuria, which is characterized by the excretion of large amounts of homogentisic acid in the urine, where it is not normally found. Because of the oxidation of the homogentisic acid, the urine turns black on exposure to the air. Alkaptanuria is often first diagnosed when a baby's wet diapers turn black. Patients with this condition are generally healthy, though later in life they appear prone to certain forms of arthritis. In his observation and experimentation, Garrod recognized that alkaptanuria was quite rare, but appeared to run in families. He noted that its mode of inheritance was consistent with Mendel's description of the inheritance of recessive traits. He believed that the disorder was the result of a disruption in one of the body's normal metabolic pathways. He supposed that the lack of an essential enzyme was responsible.

Although it took scientists another fifty years to develop the sophisticated technology necessary to prove his theory, the accuracy of Garrod's model has been sustained.

Technology has continued to become more highly sophisticated and increasingly precise in its ability to serve as an effective tool in searching out the existence and causes of genetic diseases, but we still have a tremendous way to go to understand the exact mechanisms at work. Nearly three thousand diseases have been identified as being caused by single pairs of recessive genes, and presumably most are related to the production of an abnormal gene product. Many may ultimately be proven to be enzymatic in nature, such as the one described by Garrod. But searching out the root cause of a genetic disorder is an arduous task. Thus far, only a few hundred have been directly attributed to enzymes. About a hundred of these can be identified prenatally.

THE HUMAN CHROMOSOME PUZZLE

Human cytogenetics, the science that studies the number and structure of the human chromosome complement, was not of direct use to medicine until recent years. A major stumbling block that accounted in part for this science's slow development was the simple fact that scientists did not know the exact number of human chromosomes until 1956. Without accurate knowledge of the number, shape, and structure of human chromosomes, they could not make any real progress in pinpointing the relationship of chromosomes to normal and abnormal development.

The story of how scientists eventually determined the correct number of human chromosomes illustrates the often tortuous path scientific advance can take. The forward march of science doesn't always conform to the popular vision of an objective science guided simply by the analysis of hard facts. Sometimes scientists display a great reluctance to believe their own observations when they contradict accepted theory and practice.

Human chromosomes were first observed in the late nineteenth century. But at that time most researchers focused on the behavior of chromosomes at various moments in the life of the cell, rather than on a descriptive study of chromosome structure and number. They did not fully understand the importance of chromosomes in the hereditary process, and the laboratory techniques available to them at the time were comparatively primitive. Indeed, looking at the material the early geneticists had to work with at the turn of the century, many scientists today express amazement that their predecessors were able to understand anything they saw under the microscope.

By the 1890s scientists began to realize that the behavior and function of chromosomes were consistent with the needs of the hereditary process. The chromosomes were visible in the cell nucleus only during cell division. They replicated themselves and divided to be passed on as identical sets of chromosomes to the next generation of cells. When scientists realized that chromosomes play a vital role in the passing of hereditary information from one generation of cells to the next through cell division (mitosis), and from one generation of individual organisms to the next through the production of sperm and egg cells (meiosis), they focused their attention on the study of the shape, structure, and number of chromosomes.

However, the good intentions of scientific researchers could not compensate for poor techniques and poor material. Reports on the number of chromosomes present in a normal human cell ranged from as few as eight to over fifty. In 1912 Han Van Winiwriter, a pioneer in the field of chromosome study, announced his conclusion that human females had forty-eight chromosomes, and human males forty-seven. By 1922 another prominent researcher, T. S. Painter, concluded that the correct number was either forty-eight or forty-six, regardless of sex. At first, Painter leaned toward forty-six, but he lacked the confidence to challenge the conclusions of an authority like Winiwriter, and therefore settled on forty-eight. For the next three decades, studies were published in which scientists time and time again reported that they had counted forty-eight human chromosomes in their cell samples.

T. C. Hsu, a leading American genetic researcher, points out that to reach this count of forty-eight, scientists had to force their counts. In the early 1950s Hsu developed a new technique that greatly facilitated the study of chromosomes. His technique made it easier to determine accurately the precise number of chromosomes in human cells. But Hsu consistently refused to believe his own eyes. He forced himself to mistake parts of chromosomes for separate chromosomes so that he would come up with the accepted total of forty-eight. He admits in retrospect that this error was the greatest embarrassment in his career.

In 1955 two researchers, Jo Hin Tjio and Alfred Levan, concluded that the exact number of human chromosomes was forty-six. But even they hesitated to challenge the traditionally accepted forty-eight. They published a paper in which they said that there were definitely forty-six chromosomes in the cells of the tissue they had studied, and they meekly suggested that it was likely that the same chromosome number would be found in all cells of the human body. It was a scenario reminiscent of "The Emperor's New Clothes." Once someone had the courage to say that the emperor was naked as the day he was born, other scientists began to confirm that they, too, had been counting only forty-six chromosomes in human cells. By 1956 a new scientific fact was established: the human cell has a normal complement of forty-six chromosomes.

The field of cytogenetics might never have been of interest to medical science, however, had it not been for the discovery in 1959 that Down syndrome was associated with an abnormality in the chromosomes. Patients with Down syndrome suffer severe mental retarda-

The discovery that Down syndrome was consistently associated with an abnormality in the chromosomes was the spark for the dramatic development of the science known as cytogenetics, which studies the number and structure of the chromosomes. Chromosome study involves making a karyotype: a standardized arrangement of the chromosomes from a single cell which have been photographed with microscopic enlargement of about 1250 times. The karyotype of a Down syndrome patient, in addition to the normal twenty-three pairs of chromosomes, has an extra No. 21 chromosome.

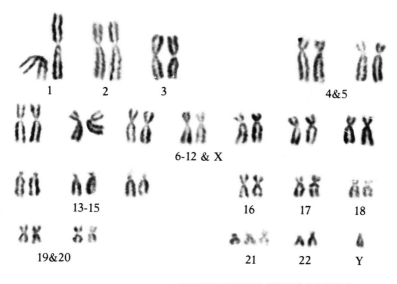

KARYOTYPE OF A MALE WITH TRISOMY 21
OR DOWN SYNDROME

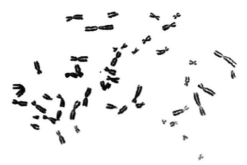

Figure 1

(Courtesy of the Cytogenetics Laboratory, NYU Medical Center)

tion and are often prone to defects of the eyes, ears, and heart as well. Instead of the normal complement of twenty-three pairs of chromosomes, Down's patients have an extra No. 21 chromosome, for a total of forty-seven chromosomes. Previously scientists had believed that abnormalities involving such a significantly large chunk of genetic information as a whole chromosome would be so disruptive to normal development that they would prove lethal during prenatal development. They were clearly wrong. The medical interest in the study of chromosomes escalated sharply.

MEDICAL USES OF GENETIC EVALUATION

The medical applications for genetic evaluation have increased dramatically in the past two decades. Many hospital departments and medical specialists routinely refer patients for genetic evaluation to make or confirm diagnoses and to aid in making decisions about treatment.

Sometimes newborn infants or young children exhibit physical or behavioral characteristics associated with chromosomal or biochemical abnormalities. If a chromosomal abnormality is suspected, appropriate genetic evaluation not only can confirm the diagnosis but also can help determine if other family members should be tested as well. In the case of a metabolic disorder, testing may identify the exact nature of the problem so that appropriate treatment, dietary restraints, and/or food supplements can be planned by the neonatologist or pediatrician.

Patients with certain types of leukemia (cancer of the blood) are often referred for chromosomal evaluation. Specific variations from the normal chromosome pattern may confirm the diagnosis of leukemia. They may even pinpoint precisely which type of leukemia is involved. Sometimes these chromosomal changes confirm that the disease has entered into a dormant stage, known as a period of remission, in which symptoms subside, or that it has entered an acute stage, where more vigorous treatment might be required.

When sexual identity or development is unclear or abnormal, a combination of chromosomal and hormonal evaluations may be appropriate to determine the chromosomal sex, the nature of the developmental disturbance, and possibilities for treatment.

Chromosomal analysis may be useful in evaluating the causes of spontaneous abortions and infertility when other explanations fail.

Some of the detrimental effects of chemical pollutants and other environmental agents can be monitored through various methods of genetic evaluation. Geneticists can aid in determining whether substances might cause changes in the genes (mutagens), cause cancer (carcinogens), or cause birth defects (teratogens).

The most dramatic medical use of genetics today is in prenatal diagnosis in cases in which the family or pregnancy is considered at risk for genetic disorders if it falls into a category which has a statistically significant greater likelihood for producing a child with a genetic disease or birth defect. Pregnant women who are at risk for bearing children with birth defects are referred for amniocentesis. In this procedure, a doctor extracts from the uterus a sample of amniotic fluid. This amniotic fluid contains some of the unborn baby's cells, and thus chromosomal or biochemical studies of the cells can examine the possibility of certain specific abnormalities in the baby.

Amniocentesis is recommended for all pregnant women over thirty-five, for those who have already had a baby with a chromosomal abnormality, for those who have a family history of such disorders, for those known to be carriers of a sex-linked disease, and for those at risk for any of approximately a hundred biochemical disorders. Genetic counselors work with the families involved, explaining the nature of any defects detected. In cases of severe birth defects, families have the option of a therapeutic abortion, after which they can try again for a normal baby. When a birth defect is not so serious or when religious beliefs or other personal considerations rule out therapeutic abortion as an option, amniocentesis at least eliminates the shock and surprise of giving birth to a baby with birth defects and allows the family to begin the necessary therapy and counseling at the appropriate moment.

As you might expect, the rapidly escalating demand for genetic evaluation by the medical profession has gone hand in hand with a rapid expansion of genetic services across the country. Thirty years ago there were only ten qualified genetic counselors in America, and their ability to serve patients was severely limited by the low level of technology at that time. Today, however, there are more than four hundred fully staffed and equipped genetics laboratories across the nation, and that number is constantly increasing. These laboratories offer a broad variety of diagnostic tests. They can determine chromosomal abnormalities with increasing subtlety, and they can identify perhaps one hundred biochemical birth defects prenatally. Many biochemical tests are so highly specialized that only one or two labs are equipped to handle them, but other procedures, particularly cytogenetics, examining the gross structural characteristics and number of chromosomes, are performed on a routine basis in most genetics laboratories.

THE LIMITS OF MEDICAL GENETICS

Genetic evaluation is today an important medical tool, but it has its limits. Genetic research literally moves along hand in hand with clinical work. New genetic disorders are discovered all the time, as doctors and laboratory researchers discover new relationships between clinically observed symptoms and genetic abnormalities. Improvements in laboratory techniques increase the ability of the laboratories to help the physician and the patient, and to unravel more of the mystery of heredity.

But the limits on genetic evaluation involve more than simple technical questions. Our theoretical understanding of heredity is still woefully incomplete. Normal and abnormal chromosomes can be identified under the microscope, and sometimes we can be certain that there is a direct relationship between a given chromosomal abnormality and a birth defect, but we don't really know why. We don't really understand what variability in chromosome shape and structure is compatible with normal development, or what variations in protein and enzyme production controlled by the genes is compatible with normal development.

Many congenital defects are genetic, but the way they are transmitted from one generation to the next is not clear. They are not reflected in identifiable changes in the shape and structure of chromosomes, and they have not been connected to specific biochemical alterations.

Many mysteries still remain, but perhaps the greatest limitation on medical genetics is that geneticists can do nothing to "cure" genetic disease. Indeed, in most cases, there isn't even a treatment that can be recommended to alleviate the symptoms of genetic disease. For a few genetic diseases such as sickle-cell anemia and phenylketonuria (PKU) there are treatments that enable a patient to function more or less normally. But there is as yet nothing to cure or eliminate these diseases. Experts can sometimes identify and describe in precise detail the tiny piece of chromosomal material responsible for the genetic disease. They can give sound advice to parents who are at risk of bearing children with genetic disorders. They can even determine whether an unborn baby suffers from a genetic disease. But they can do nothing to help the child born with extra chromosomal material.

Scientists don't yet know how the disruption of the normal genetic control mechanisms of human development works, or how they can modify that disruption, or at least alleviate the symptoms. It is a source of tremendous frustration. But the future still holds the possibility of further progress in solving the remaining puzzles and of being able to help the victims of genetic disease in a more positive way. The medical uses of genetics have come a long way in a very short time, and there is every reason to believe that progress will continue.

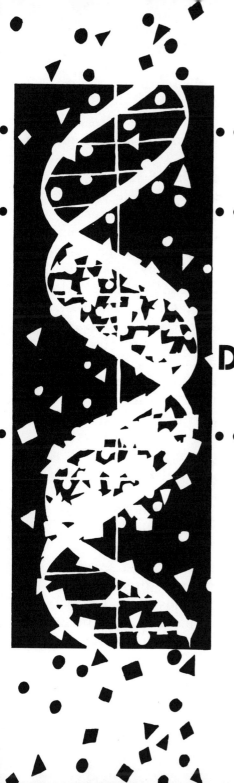

2

The
Genetic
Control of
Development

Before going on to discuss the nature of genetic disease and what happens when things go wrong in the hereditary process, it is necessary to take a brief look at the nature of normal genetic control of life.

The cell is the basic unit of life, and it is a very busy unit, whether it is a single cell organism or a cell that is part of a larger organism comprising billions of cells. Cells contain many substructures that execute specific tasks necessary for the maintenance of life. These functions are not carried out haphazardly but in a definite, controlled manner based on the interaction between the environment and the genetic program. The genetic material that contains this crucial information necessary for the normal operation and functioning of the cell is found in the nucleus. As the organism develops from a single fertilized egg cell to an adult human being made up of millions of cells, these cells must divide again and again to make more cells. It is essential that the total package of genetic information be accurately reproduced and passed on each time this happens.

THE CHROMOSOMES

The *physical* basis for accomplishing this task of reproduction is the chromosomes. The genetic information does not just float around at random in the nucleus. The nucleus is too tiny and the genetic material too vital to the maintenance of life for such chaos to exist in the cell. Nature needs a way to arrange and concentrate these strings of genes in a workable, logical fashion. If all the genetic material contained in a typical cell were stretched out, it would probably measure three feet in length. Yet nature has miraculously managed to cram this three-foot length into a cell with a diameter less than one-thousandth of an inch.

Genetic material assumes different forms at different times in the life cycle of the cell. Sometimes it appears as diffuse amorphous granules and threads called chromatin. When cells prepare to divide, each segment of genetic material, or gene, produces a replica of itself and contracts into squat rodlike chromosomes. These changes in the genetic material are not random or purposeless. The contraction of chromatin into chromosomes helps ensure the accurate separation of genetic information during cell division.

Each species has a characteristic number and structure of chromosomes. Each gene is assigned a specific location on a specific chromosome. Human beings have a normal complement of twenty-three pairs of chromosomes, for a total of forty-six. One of each pair originates from each parent.

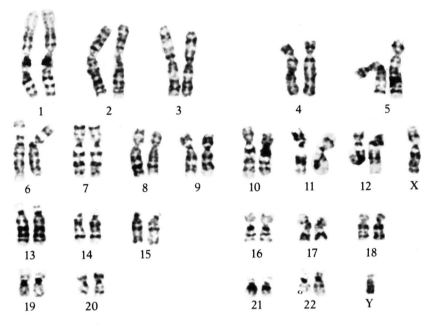

KARYOTYPE OF A NORMAL MALE

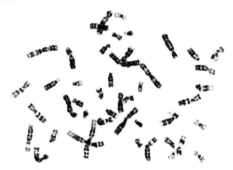

CHROMOSOMES OF A DIVIDING MALE CELL

Figure 2

(Courtesy of the Cytogenetics Laboratory, NYU Medical Center)

In order to maintain the chromosome number in each species and thereby ensure that all the genetic material is passed on intact from one generation to the next, nature has developed two different types of cell division, or reproduction. One of these cell divisions, called mitosis, is responsible for the reproduction and transmission of a complete set of genetic information to the daughter, or descendant, cells, as occurs in the growth of multicellular organisms from a single fertilized egg cell. The second type, called meiosis, produces the gametes, the sperm and egg cells, which carry only half the complete set of genetic material. The full complement of the species' characteristic chromosome number is restored when fertilization occurs, when sperm and egg unite during sexual reproduction. A brief description of these two different but indispensable types of cell division is necessary.

MITOSIS

Mitosis is the cell division that maintains the chromosome number within a living thing after fertilization occurs. It is responsible for normal body growth and development. Prior to cell division, as we have already noted, the genetic material duplicates itself, gene by gene. At the same time, the chromatin begins to contract to form the chromosomes, and the nuclear membrane separating the nucleus from the cytoplasm disappears. By the time chromosomes become visible, duplication has already been completed. Under the microscope we see duplicated, identical chromosomes, joined together at a single spot, called the centromere. The double chromosomes now move toward the center of the cell in a completely random manner. Corresponding chromosomes, carrying the matching genes for each pair, line up independently of each other. At the same time, two substructures in the cytoplasm, called centrioles, migrate toward opposite ends of the cell and begin generating fibers, which fan out toward the chromosomes in the center of the cell. The fibers soon attach themselves to the centromere, which joins the duplicated chromosomes. The fibers contract and pull the chromosomes apart and toward opposite ends of the cell until half of each duplicated chromosome has been collected around each centriole. A nuclear membrane begins to form around the chromosomes. The chromosomes lose their shape and resume their diffuse chromatin form. A pinching action snips the cytoplasm in two, and a new cell membrane forms to encircle the cytoplasm and its new nucleus. Two daughter cells with identical copies of the genetic code have been produced. Mitosis is complete (see Figure 3).

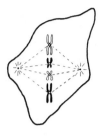

Chromosomes double in preparation for division.

Doubled chromosomes contracted and identifiable.

Doubled chromosomes line up randomly.

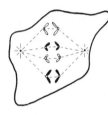

Centromeres divide and chromosomes separate.

Equal daughter cells begin to form.

Formation of two equal daughter cells completed.

Mitosis

Figure 3

MEIOSIS

Meiosis is the cell division that guarantees the maintenance of the chromosome number when sexual reproduction takes place. Meiosis does this by producing gametes that carry only a single set of chromosomes—one of each chromosome pair.

Like mitosis, the chromosomal material replicates and concentrates itself into doubled chromosomes joined at the centromere. Unlike mitosis, however, the chromosomes do not line up randomly in reduction division. Instead, as they contract, chromosomes carrying matching genes seek each other out and wrap around each other, in a process called synapsis. The chromosomes unwrap by the time they reach the center of the cell, but they line up next to each other, rather than randomly.

The fibers radiating from the centrioles pull the pairs of doubled chromosomes apart and toward opposite ends of the cell. The two daughter cells produced at this stage of meiosis have already had the total number of chromosomes reduced. Each carries only one doubled chromosome from each pair—or two copies of half the genetic material of the mother cell.

After a brief pause, each daughter cell goes through another division that is essentially mitotic in nature, producing a total of four daughter cells in all, each with one copy of half of the genetic material of the original mother cell (see Figure 4).

Chromosomes double in preparation for division.

Doubled and paired chromosomes contract.

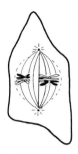

Paired chromosomes line up on opposite sides of equator.

Chromosome pairs separate.

Daughter cells have half the original number of chromosomes.

Meiosis: Reduction Division

Figure 4

THE GENETIC PROGRAM IN OPERATION

As we have said, the genetic program, which is passed on intact from generation to generation by means of the chromosomes, provides information to the cells on how to function and develop. In addition, the environment provides to the genetic program, through a system of feedback, the information it needs to trigger responses and differentiation at the appropriate time.

In higher forms of life the interaction between the environment and the genetic program is even more intricate and dependent on accurate feedback. The development of a human being from a fertilized egg is a complex process. This development must follow a definite sequential pattern. It produces very precise arrangements of the highly specialized cells that make up the body organs, tissues, and nerves. Genetic information needed at one stage of differentiation may not be needed later on, when new information will be activated. Information on the construction of an eye, for example, is translated into action before birth, not at ten years of age. As embryonic development proceeds, cells increasingly become differentiated. Unnecessary segments of the genetic program in particular cells are deactivated or turned off. Skin cells don't have to translate the same information as brain cells, but they certainly need to use the part of the code that carries information about pigmentation, gland formation, repair, and so forth.

Genetic information doesn't act directly on the life processes within the cells. It uses proteins, which act as intermediaries, to put its instructions into action. Many types of proteins can be used. One important protein group is composed of enzymes. Enzymes can initiate or speed up chemical reactions within the cells. Another group contains the structural proteins that are used to construct cartilage, bones, cell membranes, and other parts of the body. Still other proteins activate the translation of segments of the genetic program at the appropriate moment.

Proteins are manufactured in the cell cytoplasm—the material surrounding the nucleus—by linking together molecules of amino acids. There are twenty different amino acids. The exact sequence in which they are linked together determines the protein produced. Different sequential arrangements make different proteins. The genetic program carries precise instructions that guide the cell in arranging amino acids and tell the cell when to begin their production and when to terminate it.

DEOXYRIBONUCLEIC ACID (DNA)

The genetic blueprint for life is coded in a chemical substance known as deoxyribonucleic acid, or DNA. DNA is found in the nucleus of every living cell, from the simplest single cell creature to the most complex multicellular organism, and it codes the genetic program for all living things. DNA is the biochemical basis of the genetic control of development.

A gene is a segment of DNA. It contains a specific coded message that instructs the cell to produce some kind of protein which affects a characteristic of the cell or organism under the right conditions. Perhaps the coded message signals a cell substructure to produce an enzyme to control the burning of fuels and the release of energy at the appropriate moment. Perhaps the DNA message tells the cell that in response to certain stimuli or signals from cells surrounding it, or from other external sources, it will develop as part of a muscle. The DNA message will also tell the cell how to organize itself in a way characteristic of muscle cells. Or perhaps it will control the color of the organism's eyes or hair. A single human cell may have as many as 200,000 genes, each with important jobs to do, and many handling a number of responsibilities.

Physically, DNA appears as long double strands. Each strand is actually a chain of units

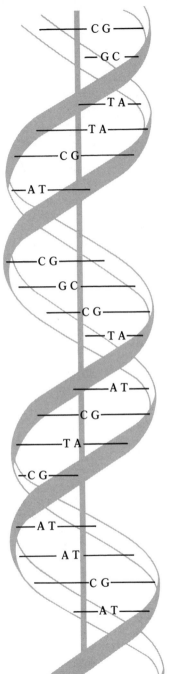

The Double Helix

Figure 5
The double helix structure of DNA is the key to the accurate replication of the genetic program, the basis for enough variation to permit evolutionary development, and a mechanism for translating the genetic program into action.

called nucleotides linked together. There are four types of nucleotides containing the bases adenine (A), cytosine (C), guanine (G), and thymine (T), which are the key to the genetic code. In much the same way as the twenty-six letters of the alphabet are used to code specific words, the precise arrangement of the nucleotides with their particular bases determines the information being communicated.

In the cell, two single DNA strands, fashioned by the chemical bonding between adjacent nucleotides in the chain, form a double-stranded helix (see Figure 5) because of the mutual attraction of each base for the corresponding base on its matching strand. These pairings are not random. They always follow a pattern. Guanine (G) always pairs with cytosine (C), and adenine (A) with thymine (T). This mutual attraction of G and C, and A and T, forms the basis for the accurate replication of DNA strands, which is required for the unaltered transmission of genetic information from one generation of cells to the next.

When a cell prepares to divide and produce two new daughter cells, the two strands of its DNA first separate and serve as models for the construction of a new strand. Since each base pairs only with its normal partner, the two new double-stranded DNA segments produced in this process are duplicates of the original DNA.

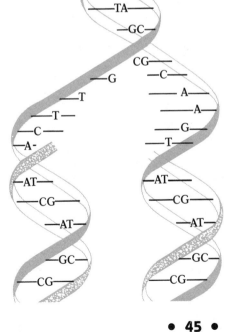

Replication of the Double Helix

Figure 6

DNA "unzips" and forms two identical helices in a process called semiconservative replication. Each new double helix contains (or conserves) one strand of bases from the original double helix and one that has been constructed by the complementary association of bases (A with T, G with C).

Before cell division occurs, the DNA in the cell nucleus has already been duplicated. When actual cell division occurs, one copy of the identical DNA material goes to each daughter cell.

Should a mistake occur in the duplication of the DNA strands, so that one of the base pairs fails to link up with its normal partner, an incorrect piece of information can be included in the genetic code. This change in the genetic code is called a mutation. If the mutation is not so serious as to be lethal to the cell, it can be passed on to future generations of cells.

Accurate reproduction of DNA is an absolute necessity. The genetic program is duplicated each and every time a cell divides, billions of times in a human being's lifetime. Every cell except the gametes must carry a complete set of genetic information. The gametes carry only half a set. In all cases, it is essential that the cell receive an accurate copy of its genetic material. If replication is inaccurate, the genetic program may degenerate. What started out as a definite, sequentially ordered set of information would become nothing but a bunch of random nonsense.

The ability of DNA to incorporate changes has been the basis of variation through which evolution has taken place. Although single base substitutions may occur frequently, mechanisms exist to repair most of them before they reach the stabilized "altered" form.

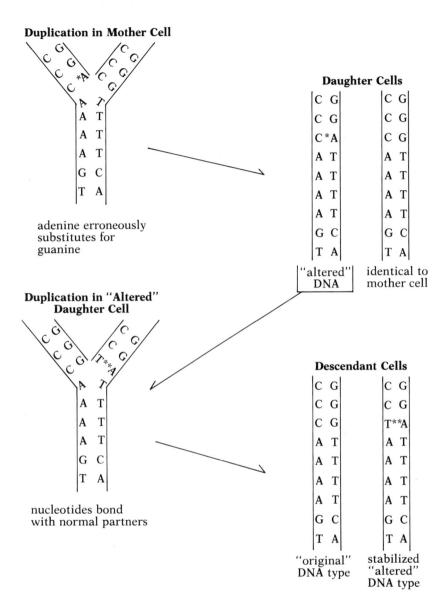

Duplication in Mother Cell

C G
C G
C *A

A T
A T
A T
G C
T A

adenine erroneously
substitutes for
guanine

Daughter Cells

C G	C G
C G	C G
C *A	C G
A T	A T
A T	A T
A T	A T
A T	A T
G C	G C
T A	T A

"altered"   identical to
DNA   mother cell

**Duplication in "Altered"
Daughter Cell**

C G
C G
C G T**A

A T
A T
A T
G C
T A

nucleotides bond
with normal partners

Descendant Cells

C G	C G
C G	C G
C G	T**A
A T	A T
A T	A T
A T	A T
A T	A T
G C	G C
T A	T A

"original"   stabilized
DNA type   "altered"
              DNA type

How Point Mutations Occur

Figure 7

This accuracy is utilized in the translation of genetic information into action in the cell. A series of three adjacent nucleotides in the DNA provides the code for a single amino acid. These combinations also signal where messages start and stop, similar to punctuation marks in a sentence. The sequence of nucleotides in a DNA strand indirectly provides the code for the sequence of amino acids in the proteins produced in the cytoplasm, which direct the living thing's development and survival (see Figure 8).

The coded information in the DNA is interpreted through a molecule called messenger RNA, which carries a copy of a selected portion of the gene segment to the cytoplasm. The messenger RNA is produced in much the same way in which the DNA replicates itself. The gene involved temporarily separates and produces a strand of messenger RNA, composed of molecules of a slightly different substance known as ribonucleic acid. The messenger RNA travels out of the nucleus to protein manufacturing sites in the cytoplasm where the sequentially ordered triplet base codes are translated into the arrangements of specified amino acids that make up specific proteins.

To sum up, the integrity and accuracy of the genetic program is maintained during cell division on the physical level by the behavior of

The Genetic Code

TRIPLET IN DNA	TRIPLET IN mRNA	AMINO ACID CODED	TRIPLET IN DNA	TRIPLET IN mRNA	AMINO ACID CODED
ATA	UAU	Tyrosine	AAA	UUU	Phenylalanine
ATG	UAC		AAG	UUC	
ATT	UAA	Termination of chain	AAT	UUA	Leucine
ATC	UAG		AAC	UUG	
GTA	CAU	Histadene	GAA	CUU	Leucine
GTG	CAC		GAG	CUC	
GTT	CAA	Glycine	GAT	CUA	
GTC	CAG		GAC	CUG	
TTA	AAU	Asparagine	TAA	AAU	Isoleucine
TTG	AAC		TAG	AUC	
TTT	AAA	Lysine	TAT	AUA	
TTC	AAG		TAC	AUG	Methionine
CTA	GAU	Aspartic acid	CAA	GUU	Valine
CTG	GAC		CAG	GUC	
CTT	GAA	Glutamic acid	CAT	GUA	
CTC	GAG		CAC	GUG	
ACA	UGU	Cystine or cystein	AGA	UCU	Serine
ACG	UGC		AGG	UCC	
ACT	UGA	Termination of chain	AGT	UCA	
ACC	UGG	Tryptophan	AGC	UCG	
GCA	CGU	Arginine	GGA	CCU	Proline
GCG	CGC		GGG	CCC	
GCT	CGA		GGT	CCA	
GCC	CGG		GGC	CCG	
TCA	AGU	Serine	TGA	ACU	Threonine
TCG	AGC		TGG	ACC	
TCT	AGA	Arginine	TGT	ACA	
TCC	AGG		TGC	AGG	
CCA	GGU	Glycine	CGA	GCU	Alanine
CCG	GGC		CGG	GGC	
CCT	GGA		CGT	GCA	
CCC	GGG		CGC	GCG	

Figure 8

specific gene unit

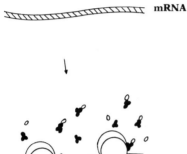 DNA

gene in DNA unzips

mRNA

by complementation single stranded mRNA formed

with slight alterations mRNA enters cytoplasm

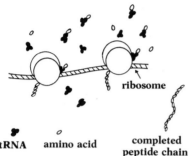

at ribosomes, tRNA coupled with specific amino acids translate DNA code into the specific sequences in proteins

ribosome

tRNA   amino acid   completed peptide chain

Protein Synthesis

Figure 9

The information coded in the DNA is transmitted to the cytoplasm in the form of messenger RNA (mRNA), which is formed as a complement to one strand of DNA. In the cytoplasm, this coded information is translated into action by means of intermediaries of transfer RNA (tRNA), which line up appropriate amino acids in specific sequence to create protein molecules.

the chromosomes and on a molecular level by the biochemical nature of DNA. When errors occur in either of these mechanisms, the genetic program may be disrupted and genetic disease may result. Genetic disease is the topic of the next chapter.

3

The Nature of Genetic Disease

In the preceding chapter we discussed the nature of genetic control of normal life functioning. A breakdown in any of these control mechanisms can result in abnormal development. Because of the complexity and diversity of the genetic control mechanism, genetic disease takes a variety of forms. As mentioned previously, these can be classified in three broad categories: single gene disorders, chromosomal abnormalities, and multifactorial disorders. In this chapter we will take a deeper look at the nature of genetic disease.

SINGLE GENE DISORDERS

The genetic program of human beings contains an estimated thirty thousand structural genes, which are responsible for the basic regulation and development of the organism. These genes control the production of certain structural proteins, which constitute the components of muscles, nerves, specialized organ tissues, blood cells, and other parts of the body. These genes also control the normal functioning of the body and its cells through the production of enzymes, which regulate the body's metabolic and biochemical functions.

As we have pointed out already, a protein is made up of a long chain of amino acids linked together in a precise sequential order, which is itself determined by the order of bases coded in the DNA in the genes. Any alteration in the arrangement of even a single base in the DNA strand may be responsible for one of a number of possible changes in the protein produced in the cell. Let's examine for a moment the possible effects a single base change in a DNA triplet code might have. For the purposes of our example, we will take the triplet code ACA (also known as a codon), which is the code for the production of the amino acid cystine. What are the possible effects of a change in the third base, an A, in this codon?

1. A change in the third base might result in no change in the protein produced, because the new code might simply be a different way of coding for the same amino acid. Thus, if the third base in our particular triplet code were replaced by a G, then instead of ACA, we would have the code ACG, which is another way of coding for the same amino acid, cystine. There would therefore be no alteration in the protein produced.
2. The change might result in a wrong amino acid being substituted in the protein chain. Thus, if the third base in our ACA code were replaced by a C, we would have the code ACC, which is the code for the amino acid tryptophan. This would mean that tryptophan would appear in the protein chain instead of cystine. The impact of this amino acid

substitution would depend on the nature of the amino acid involved and whether it appears in a critical or active site in the protein chain. The mutation might be tolerated by the organism as producing a variant protein still permitting normal functioning, or it might produce a defective protein causing altered functioning, or it might produce a severely defective or unstable protein incapable of performing normal functions for the organism.

3. The change in the third base might cause a lengthening or shortening of the protein chain. Thus, if the third base in our ACA code were replaced by a T, we would have the code ACT, which is the code for terminating a chain of amino acids. This means the protein chain would be prematurely terminated, and the result could be the production of a different type of protein, which might function in a totally inappropriate way. Conversely, if the normally occurring code was indeed ACT, the signal to terminate a chain, and another base was substituted for the T, the chain would fail to end where it should, and we would have continued protein synthesis until another termination code was reached. The elongated protein produced in this variation might also impair the normal functioning of the organism.

4. The impact of the change in a single base in the triplet code also depends on the particular region within the gene in which such a change might occur. If the alteration happens outside the area coding for the protein itself, but in the gene regulatory area, the normal production of protein synthesis might be disrupted. Even though the code for the protein itself might still be accurate, it

might be impossible to start and stop the protein synthesis correctly. Inappropriate levels of protein production or timing could result.

STRUCTURAL ABNORMALITIES

Sickle-cell anemia. You have probably heard of the disease called sickle-cell anemia. This disease occurs most frequently among people descended from residents of equatorial Africa, but it also affects people from the Mediterranean region and the Indian subcontinent. About 0.25 percent of American blacks are born with sickle-cell anemia. The red blood cells of victims of this disease become abnormal in shape under certain conditions, hence the name "sickle cell." The clinical symptoms include anemia and jaundice (yellowing of the skin). Patients may undergo certain crisis periods during which blood vessels become blocked by collapsed cells. This causes a painful loss of blood supply to bones, spleen, lungs, and other body organs. The parents of affected children are clinically normal, but are carriers of the sickle-cell trait, which is inherited in a manner typical of a recessive gene. Under laboratory conditions, some of the parents' blood cells can be forced to take on the sickle shape, and this fact can be used as a test to determine which families are most likely to bear children with sickle-cell disease.

The cause of this disease is an abnormality in the hemoglobin molecule in the blood, which is controlled by a mutation in a single gene pair. Hemoglobin is the structural protein found in the red blood cells of vertebrates (animals with backbones). It is responsible for transporting oxygen to the cells of the body. Several different types of hemoglobin function at different periods in the life of the organism. The production of these different types is controlled by the genetic program that turns production on and off at the appropriate moment in the life cycle. Hemoglobin molecules are made up of chains of as many as 146 amino acids.

Sickle-cell anemia is caused specifically by a single amino acid substitution of valine for glutamine in the sixth position on one of the chains. This seemingly minor alteration is responsible for all the clinical symptoms of the disease. The change is caused by an alteration in the DNA code. The carriers of the sickle-cell trait have one gene for a normal hemoglobin chain and one gene for an abnormal chain. The sickle-cell patient is an offspring of two parents who are carriers and has inherited the gene for abnormal hemoglobin from both parents. The child therefore has no genes for the normal hemoglobin chain. Advances in medical practice have gone a long way toward easing the suffering of sickle-cell patients, but nothing as yet has been done to cure or eliminate the disease.

As you might imagine, in a molecule made up of so many amino acids strung together, many other variations from the normal configuration of hemoglobin are possible. Indeed scientists have observed over 220 variations in the hemoglobin chains. Most appear to be tolerated by the organism, however, and do not cause agonizing illness like sickle-cell anemia.

Up to now, we have been examining the possible impact of a change in just one base in a single triplet DNA code. However, things can get much more complicated. Larger alterations, such as the duplication, deletion, or spatial rearrangement of larger portions of a single gene, involving hundreds and hundreds of triplet codes, are possible.

Thalassemia is another hemoglobin disease that you might have heard of. It takes several forms, but none results from structural defects or alterations in the hemoglobin molecule. The disease is caused by a defect in the rate of synthesis of the hemoglobin. This defect is the result of a deletion of one or both of the genes controlling hemoglobin production.

INBORN ERRORS OF METABOLISM

Genetic defects called inborn errors of metabolism function at a different level than do the defects in structural proteins we have discussed previously. Rather than affecting the way the body is constructed—the way cells are formed, for example—these defects affect the body's metabolism, or the way the body processes fuel into energy and cellular products. These biochemical diseases are caused by a genetic defect in the production of enzymes that blocks the normal way in which the organism breaks down and uses the nutrients to build what it needs. An enzyme is a protein that controls or expedites the biochemical changes and reactions within the cells.

The metabolic processes consist of a series of sequential biochemical reactions following a definite pathway. Each reaction in a given pathway is aided by the action of a specific enzyme that helps convert a molecule from one form (the substrate) into another (the product). The product of one step in the pathway becomes the substrate for the next step and is acted upon by still another enzyme to be converted into another product, and so on down the line until the final end product is created. While the type of conversion taking place at each step in the process varies, each enzyme is specific for each substrate, each conversion process, and each product.

Changes in enzymes are usually the result of a single base substitution in the genetic code, but may also be caused by deletions and rearrangements of genetic material. Such changes result in alterations in the shape of the enzyme, in its ability to join with a substance known as a coenzyme (usually a vitamin and often the active portion of the enzyme), or in its ability to recognize and interact with the substrate. Any of these results would obviously make the enzyme less effective, or ineffective, in helping to carry out the necessary chemical reaction in the cell. Other mutations may result in a lowered production of, or even a total absence of, the necessary enzyme. In any case there would be a partial or total block on the metabolic pathway.

Blocks in a metabolic pathway may negatively affect the individual by causing

- an absence of a necessary end product
- an overaccumulation of an unnecessary intermediate product
- production of a toxic waste product not usually found in the body (see Figure 10).

The clinical symptoms of inborn errors of metabolism may be quite diverse and unexpected. Many take the form of degenerative diseases that attack multiple organ systems in the body. This broadly ranging impact on patients often makes it difficult to determine which enzyme is involved. If the enzyme defect responsible can be identified, however, it is

The metabolic processes of the body consist of a stepwise series of reactions. The reactions in the pathway are aided by specific enzymes, which convert a molecule from one form (the substrate) into another (the product). The product of one step becomes the substrate for the next step, in which it is acted upon by another enzyme and converted into another product. This process continues until the end product of the pathway is reached. The conversion involved may consist of changing a chemical bond, adding or deleting atoms from a molecule, joining two molecules together, splitting a molecule, and so forth. Each enzyme is specific for the substrate, conversion process, and product.

The diagram represents a generalized metabolic pathway. A transport enzyme, T_A, is needed to bring the starting substrate across the cell membrane into the cell. In the cell this substrate is normally converted into product B, then into product C, and finally into end product D, with the assistance of the appropriate enzymes E_{AB}, E_{BC}, and E_{CD} along the pathway.

A deficiency in any of these enzymes can result in problems because of the lack of the end product or an abnormal accumulation of an intermediary product.

The accumulation of A may open an alternate metabolic pathway to eliminate this accumulation. If either product F or product G is toxic, problems can result.

If the feedback mechanism fails to function properly, too much or too little of the end product D may be produced.

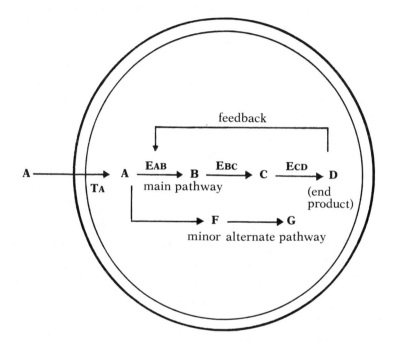

Metabolic Pathways and Genetic Disease

Figure 10

sometimes possible for medical science to intervene, modify the environment of the patient, and thereby avoid some of the most harmful consequences of the disorder.

An example is the disease known as PKU (phenylketonuria). Newborn babies in the United States are routinely screened for PKU by means of a blood test at birth. PKU is a serious disease, which, if untreated, can result in severe mental retardation. The disease is caused by a defect in the production of phenylalanine hydroxylase, an enzyme that plays a key role in the metabolic process breaking down phenylalanine, an amino acid found in many proteins, so that it can be used by the body. Because the body is unable to process it in the normal way, there is an abnormal accumulation of phenylalanine in the body of a PKU baby. This causes the body to shift to alternate ways of metabolizing the amino acid, and the end result is a large buildup of toxic products not normally found in the body. These toxic substances are responsible for the retardation associated with the disease. PKU is caused by a recessive mutation in the phenylalanine hydroxylase gene. At birth PKU babies are healthy because their mother's enzyme system has protected them during the prenatal period. The symptoms of the disease develop later on.

The impact of the disease can be avoided by means of a special diet low in phenylalanine. For a PKU patient, doctors must determine a diet that carefully balances low phenylalanine levels with the need for this nutrient for normal development. After three years of age the human brain is generally stabilized enough so that it is no longer as vulnerable to the effects of PKU, and the diet restrictions can begin to be relaxed. Recent evidence shows that PKU mothers must return to the controlled diet during all of their pregnancies or their babies will be born mentally retarded. This will happen not because of any PKU disease in the babies, but because the enzyme deficiency in the mother will create an unhealthy prenatal environment for the baby.

A special type of single gene disorder involves genes located on the sex chromosomes—those chromosomes that determine the genetic sex of the individual. Twenty-two of the twenty-three pairs of chromosomes found in human cells are to be found in either male or female cells. But the twenty-third pair, the sex chromosomes, is different. In females this pair is composed of two large chromosomes, called X chromosomes (Figure 11). In males, however, this pair is composed of only one X chromosome and a small truncated chromosome called the Y chromosome. Except

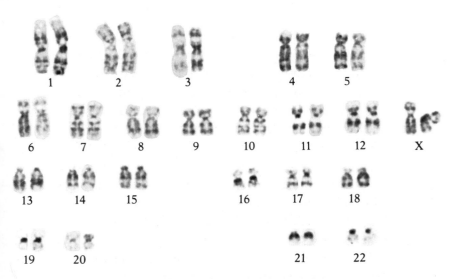

KARYOTYPE OF A NORMAL FEMALE

CHROMOSOMES OF A DIVIDING FEMALE CELL
Figure 11

(Courtesy of the Cytogenetics Laboratory, NYU Medical Center)

for some genes associated with male development, very few genes are known to be located
on the Y chromosome. If there are any, such
traits would be passed on from father to son.

This chromosome difference between males
and females has some important implications
for genetic disease. It means that the expression of any gene located on the X chromosome
will be different in males and females. Because
males have only one X chromosome, any gene
on that chromosome, including an abnormal
gene, will be expressed with no modification.
Although only one X chromosome is active in
any given cell in females, the expression of an
abnormal gene on one X chromosome in a
female is modified by the activity of the corresponding normal gene on the other chromosome in surrounding cells.

An X-linked recessive disease, such as
hemophilia or certain forms of muscular dys-
trophy, is usually inherited by a son from his
mother who is an unaffected carrier. She carries the abnormal gene on one of her X
chromosomes. The expression of the abnormal
gene in the mother is masked by the normal
gene on her other X chromosomes. Her
daughters might be completely normal, or they
could be carriers like their mother. In the carrier daughters, the abnormal gene on the X
chromosome inherited from the mother would

be masked by the normal gene located on the X chromosome contributed by the father's sperm. But in the son, the abnormal gene would express itself because nothing on the Y chromosome would compensate for the effects of the abnormal gene. Such diseases are called X-linked, or sex-linked, diseases.

CHROMOSOMAL ABNORMALITIES

The genetic diseases we have discussed so far involve a harmful change in the DNA code, which leads to an abnormal gene product. This is not so in the genetic diseases caused by chromosomal abnormalities. Chromosomal abnormalities involve changes, not in the basic information coded in the DNA, but rather its balance or arrangement. There may be either too much or too little of a particular segment of code, or it may be in the wrong place.

The first proven link between abnormal chromosomes and abnormal development occurred in 1959 when Lejeune discovered that patients suffering from Down syndrome had an extra small chromosome. Chromosome abnormalities are now known to be far more common and varied than anyone originally believed possible, and are a significant cause of birth defects and prenatal death. In fact, 50 percent of all miscarriages are attributable to chromosomal abnormalities. Such abnormalities are believed to affect 7.5 percent of all babies conceived and 0.7 percent of all babies born alive. Most chromosome imbalances prove fatal to the unborn child and cause spontaneous abortion within the first three months of pregnancy.

Because they involve comparatively large segments of genetic material and therefore constitute a sizable disruption of the genetic balance, chromosomal abnormalities in general share certain common features. Most are characterized by abnormally slow growth, mental retardation, somewhat abnormal physical appearance, and a disruption of multiple organ systems. In addition, these disorders are characterized by particular, recognizable symptoms that relate in some as yet unknown way to the specific genes found in the missing or extra material.

As mechanisms for ensuring the correct transmission of genetic information on a physical level, chromosomes are integral to the process of duplicating, sorting, and dividing the genetic material. As in any such process, mistakes are possible. Sometimes whole chromosomes go to the wrong place. Sometimes the chromosomes get tangled up in each other and break. Broadly speaking two categories of chromosome abnormality are

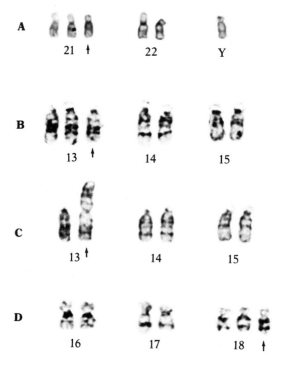

Figure 12

found routinely in the laboratory: numerical errors and structural errors.

Numerical errors. Numerical chromosome abnormalities can occur either in mitosis, the cell division responsible for body growth, or in meiosis, the cell division responsible for the production of the gametes, when a whole chromosome fails to separate normally from its partner (nondysjunction). The result is that one daughter cell is missing a whole chromosome and one daughter cell has an extra chromosome. In general missing chromosomes are fatal to the affected cell.

If such an error in cell division occurs in a gamete, then all the cells in the fetus will have the same abnormal chromosome pattern. If the error occurs after fertilization in a mitotic division, only some of the cells will be abnormal.

Few chromosome trisomies, except for the sex chromosomes, can survive until birth. Those that do are associated with multiple abnormalities and mental retardation:

A Trisomy 21—Down syndrome
B Trisomy 13—Patau syndrome
C Familial or translocation trisomy 13 in which two No. 13 chromosomes are linked and move together during meiosis
D Trisomy 18—Edward's syndrome

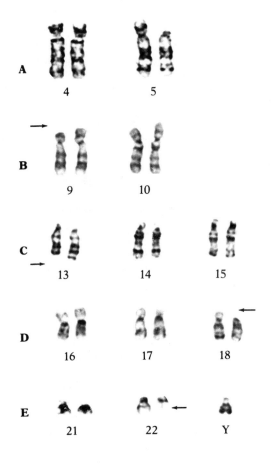

Figure 13

This mixture of normal and abnormal cells in one individual is called mosaicism.

Structural abnormalities. Chromosomes break and reattach often. Most of the time they reattach to the same place and the event goes undetected. Sometimes the reattachment does not occur and a piece of the genetic material is lost. Occasionally more than one chromosome

Loss of an entire chromosome, except for a sex chromosome, is seen only rarely in living individuals. Deletions of portions of chromosomes have been seen, and some of these deletions have been associated with identifiable clinical syndromes. The loss of chromosomal material is extremely disruptive to the balance of cellular function and development. Such deletions are therefore often associated with congenital abnormalities affecting multiple organ systems and mental retardation. In addition, the loss of some chromosomal material may permit the expression of specific detrimental recessive genes on the remaining chromosome; the effects of these genes would normally have been masked. This may explain why missing chromosomes are often lethal.

Seen in Figure 13 are deletions of:

    A The short arm of the No. 5 chromosome (cri du chat syndrome)
    B The short arm of the No. 9 chromosome
    C Part of the long arm of the No. 13 chromosome
    D The short arm of chromosome No. 18
    E Chromosome No. 22 long arm, called the Philadelphia chromosome (found in some forms of leukemia)

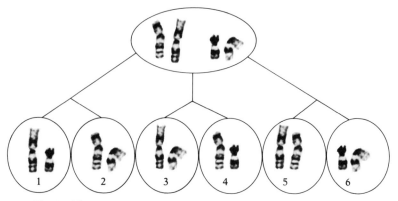

Figure 14
Meiosis with a Balanced Translocation

Apparently balanced inherited translocations seem to be compatible with completely normal development in some cases. The risk of producing abnormalities centers on the formation of gametes (eggs or sperm). In the production of the gametes during meiosis, rearranged chromosomes may separate in a way that results in a higher than normal frequency of unbalanced gametes. If fertilized, these unbalanced gametes may produce nonviable or abnormal fetuses.

The top line of the figure shows the No. 1 and No. 11 chromosome pairs of an adult with a balanced translocation of one chromosome of each pair. Because this is a balanced translocation, the adult is normal and healthy.

The bottom line of the figure represents six theoretically possible gametes that can be produced during meiosis by the separation of the two translocated chromosome pairs (other chromosomes would be normal). Because of the rearrangement, meiotic separation does not always occur normally. Gamete No. 1 would be normal, with no translocation involved. Gamete No. 2 would be a balanced translocation, just like the parent. If fertilized, the individual would probably be normal like the parent. Possible gametes No. 3 through No. 6 would all be abnormal, having either too much or too little of certain chromosomal material. If fertilized, abnormalities or fetal death would presumably result.

breaks at one time and they reattach erroneously, swapping places.

The results of these breaks and reattachments may include deletion (when a chromosome segment is missing), duplication (when a
chromosome segment is repeated), inversion
(when part of the chromosome is upside down),
and translocation (when parts of chromosomes
swap places).

Sometimes structural rearrangements, especially if they involve extra or missing genetic
material, are as harmful as the numerical abnormalities. However, the impact of misplaced
material can vary. If no material is lost or
gained, the individual may develop completely
normally.

MULTIFACTORIAL INHERITANCE

Many traits are controlled not simply by a
single gene pair, but by the mutual interaction
of a number of genes, and their expression is
influenced by environmental conditions. Multifactorial inheritance is determined either by
many genes, each of which makes a small con-
tribution to the final form of the trait, or by a
major gene acting with minor genes, each of
which exerts a lesser influence on the trait.
These traits include intelligence (as measured
by IQ tests), height, and fingerprints. Multifac-

torial inheritance explains a large amount of normal human variation, but sometimes the accumulative effects of many genes can push the expression of this variation beyond the limits of normal development. A number of congenital malformations can be attributed to multifactorial inheritance, though the specific influence and activity of the genes involved are not yet known. These birth defects include cleft lip and cleft palate, club foot, and spina bifida (incomplete closure of the spine).

Because so many different types of genetic disease are possible, many different methods and techniques are used in genetic evaluation. In the next chapter we will explore some of these methods and the problems involved in their use.

4

The Tools
of Genetic
Evaluation

The first problem encountered by the physician diagnosing a patient possibly suffering from a genetic disorder is to determine if the problem really is genetic. Many disorders caused primarily by environmental factors appear similar to genetic disease, and it is necessary to differentiate between the two kinds of diseases in order to diagnose and treat the patient correctly.

The first step is a complete physical examination by a highly skilled syndromologist who is trained not only to look at individual symptoms but also to pay attention to and recognize when a cluster of individual clinical findings fits together, suggesting a specific genetic and/or chromosomal abnormality. The syndromologist undertakes the physical examination with a tape measure in hand and an eye for very detailed observation.

The patient's height and weight are noted and compared with the norms for age and sex. Head and facial features are often crucial clues to genetic disease. Abnormalities in the size and shape of the head, the shape and position of the ears, the distance between the eyes, the shape of eyelids and details of eye structure, the shape of the nose and nostrils, the shape of the mouth and the presence of clefts of the lip and/or palate may be indicators of genetic disorders. Abnormalities of the hands and feet including their shape and size, the size, shape, and quality of the fingernails, and the ridges in finger-, hand-, and footprints have been observed in several genetic syndromes as well. Abnormalities of the heart, circulation, blood pressure, and a multitude of internal organs (spleen, liver, kidney, bladder, intestines, stomach, and so forth) may be associated with genetic disease. Development delays or the failure of the patient to meet or retain developmental milestones in infancy or various levels of mental retardation may be associated with biochemical and chromosomal abnormalities.

Observation of a specific clinical feature is not enough for diagnosis. The whole picture presented by the clinical features can raise suspicions in the doctor's mind. But more is needed for an accurate diagnosis. A complete family history is required to determine if the traits that seemed abnormal in the examination of the patient are really abnormalities or are just family resemblances that the child normally inherited. (A short family, for example, will likely produce a small child.) If the whole family has low-set ears or short stubby fingers or close-set eyes, these features become less significant elements in the clinical picture.

The family history may also confirm the cluster of symptoms if they occur in other family members. By questioning the family about the same features in members of past generations a particular type of inheritance pattern (recessive, dominant, or sex-linked, for example) may be suggested.

It must be remembered that it is not usually one specific clinically observed characteristic that points to the diagnosis of a particular biochemical or chromosomal abnormality. Many features linked to such disorders also occur among the general population, in people who are perfectly normal. Some of these features may be mimicked by traumatic events or environmental agents, yet have nothing to do with inherited genetic disease. For example, mental retardation may result from oxygen deprivation at birth. Cleft lip and/or palate may be induced by the action of certain chemicals (teratogens), and deafness may result from a prenatal infection of German measles. A skillful, intelligent interpretation of the whole clinical picture is necessary to point to the diagnosis of genetic disease.

Medical genetics is able to make this evaluation of the physical status of the patient by examining a living patient after birth and has progressed to the point where some physical diagnosis can actually take place prenatally.

Ultrasound. Ultrasound is one of the more modern techniques used in prenatal examination of the fetus. It employs sound waves to derive an accurate picture of the baby while it is in the uterus. Quick-pulsing, high-frequency, low-intensity sound waves pass through the mother's abdomen, through both the mother's and the baby's tissues. When a sound wave passes from one tissue into another of different density, some of the sound wave is reflected back like an echo to the receiver instrument. The rest of the sound wave passes on to the next tissue, where again some of it is reflected back and some passes through. The reflected waves are picked up by the transmitter/receiver instrument and converted from audio signals into electronic signals, amplified and displayed as a visual signal on a television-type monitor. In this way the physician can determine the boundaries of the uterus, the position of the placenta, the location of accessible areas for procedures like amniocentesis (in which a sample of amniotic fluid must be taken from the uterus), and the overall size and shape of the baby. A well-trained ultrasound operator can observe details of spinal structure and even the baby's arms, legs, fingers, and toes. Different types of ultrasound equipment can yield still or moving images of the baby, each of which offers different advantages and disadvantages of relative cost, mobility, and degree of accurate resolution.

Ultrasound has been particularly useful in a number of areas. It has made the amniocentesis procedure safer and more effective by localizing the placenta and the fetus before the insertion of the needle used to withdraw the amniotic fluid. It can be used in the early identification of multiple pregnancies (twins, triplets, etc.), which are considered higher risk pregnancies and require closer medical monitoring. Ultrasound can be used for diagnosing accurately the age of the fetus; this information is required for the right timing of amniocentesis and for the correct interpretation of certain biochemical tests. It can be used to detect abnormalities in the rate of fetal growth, or abnormalities in the volume of amniotic fluid which may indicate fetal abnormalities like kidney nonfunction. Ultrasound may also detect structural abnormalities— such as disproportionate limbs or head— linked to various genetic diseases. As you can see, ultrasound is a versatile tool of genetic evaluation.

X-rays. The use of X-rays in prenatal diagnosis has largely been supplanted by the ultrasound technique because of the concern about exposing mother and fetus to the potentially harmful effects of radiation. The recommended procedure today is to postpone any X-rays of pregnant women until as late as possible in the pregnancy. Safer methods, such as ultrasound, which can yield the same or similar information, are used instead whenever possible. When no alternative exists, X-rays are used in a well-planned limited manner, designed to expose the fetus to radiation as little as possible. X-rays are capable of detecting abnormalities of the head and spine, and various skeletal abnormalities such as dwarfism and bone defects.

Fetoscopy. Fetoscopy is another very new technique used in the prenatal examination of the fetus. It involves the insertion of a visualizing tube through the mother's abdominal wall into the uterus. The tube is fitted with a self-focusing lens that makes it possible for the physician to do a visual examination of the surface features of the fetus. Because the area visible at any given moment is severely restricted in size, the unequivocal identification of specific fetal parts is somewhat difficult. However, there has been success in visualizing the skin, fingers, toes, face, spine, and external genitalia (important in cases of sex-linked diseases). The success of fetoscopy is hampered by chance movements of the fetus.

The visualizing tube can be equipped with a device for taking samples of fetal skin or fetal blood. This makes possible, at least theoretically, the prenatal diagnosis of a number of biochemical and hemoglobin (sickle-cell anemia and thalassemia) disorders. Fetal blood samples can also be used as a backup for inconclusive chromosomal analyses performed following the drawing of amniotic fluid in amniocentesis.

Safety considerations. Of the three methods used for the physical examination of the fetus described here, ultrasound is considered the safest. Ultrasound is the least invasive procedure, since it does not involve penetrating the uterus with needles, tubes, or other foreign objects and is believed to be without risk for mother and baby. However, it is a new technique, and no long-term studies of its impact as yet exist. Because of the risks associated with radiation exposure, X-rays are employed only late in the pregnancy and under very controlled conditions. Because of the risks associated with entering the uterus with a fetoscope, the procedure is recommended in only a limited number of cases.

If the physical examination or the family history suggests that a genetic disorder may be involved, a biochemical evaluation or a chromosomal analysis, or both, may be suggested. What type of genetic evaluation is recommended depends on what disorder the physician suspects. The test procedures are highly specialized and quite expensive and are therefore not suggested unless some particular type of disorder is suspected.

CYTOGENETIC EVALUATION

Sometimes an examination of the number and detailed structure of the patient's chromosomes is required in order to diagnose or confirm a suspected genetic disease. The question of when such a laboratory test would be undertaken will be discussed in the next chapter. Our concern here will be to describe how cytogenetic evaluation is technically accomplished.

In most cases an individual's chromosomes are the same in every cell nucleus in the body. Therefore, studying the chromosomes from any cell source can provide the normal or "constitutional" chromosome pattern for the individual. The most convenient source of cells is the blood. Blood samples are usually drawn from a finger or vein. Occasionally, skin cells or

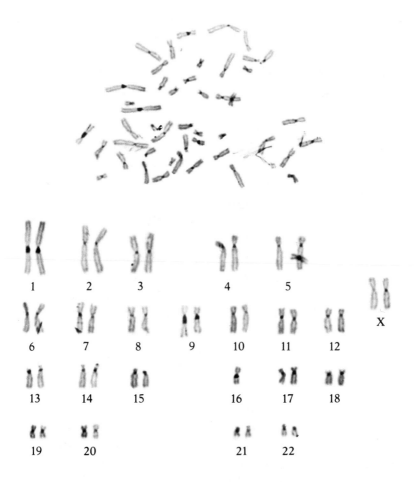

Figure 15

bone marrow cells may be used, but only in special cases.

When prenatal cytogenetic evaluation is necessary, a fetal cell source is obtained by amniocentesis. After locating the position of the placenta and the fetus, the obstetrician administers a local anesthetic and inserts a long narrow needle through the mother's abdominal wall into an unobstructed space in the uterus and withdraws a small sample of the fluid surrounding the fetus. Fetal cells floating in the amniotic fluid provide the source for chromosome analysis. Cells are taken and cultured in a supportive growth medium so that

C-Banding Analysis of Chromosomes

Consistent darkly stained regions that represent the centromeres of all chromosomes (except the Y chromosome) and variable regions on chromosomes No. 1, 9, and 16 can be elicited through special staining procedures in the laboratory. Chemically fixed chromosomes are pretreated with an alkaline solution and then a warm saline solution. They are then stained with Giema to produce the dark regions, which are known as C-bands. C-banding has only limited applications in genetic diagnosis. It can be used to determine which centromeres are involved in certain translocations, and whether variations in the structure of chromosomes No. 1, 9, and 16 are normally inherited from the parents, or are abnormal.

an adequate number of dividing cells can be collected.

A chemical that interrupts the division process is used to lock these cells in that phase of division in which the chromosomes are visible and individually identifiable. Then the cells are swollen with a diluted salt solution so that chromosomes won't be tangled up. The fixed cells are then dropped on slides, treated, and stained to help make the internal structure of the chromosomes more visible. The cells are examined and photographed under the microscope at an enlargement of about 1,250 times, and then the photographs themselves are enlarged from 4 to 10 times. Individual chromosomes are then cut and arranged in a manner established by international agreement of geneticists throughout the world; this arrangement is called a karyotype.

Another technique for detecting birth defects prenatally may someday replace amniocentesis. Known as chorionic villus biopsy, this procedure involves the taking of a sample of tiny protrusions from the chorionic membrane which surrounds the fetus and eventually becomes part of the placenta. Since this tissue is fetal in origin, a genetic analysis of the biopsy material reveals genetic information about the fetus. The procedure has been used in China and in Europe, and it is currently under investigation for use in the United States. Its advantages over amniocentesis include the fact that the procedure can be performed earlier in the pregnancy, that it is a less risky procedure since the material can be extracted through the vaginal opening rather than through the abdominal wall, and that the cells are rapidly dividing ones and hence no cell culturing is necessary. Expectant parents can receive the results within one week as compared to the three to four weeks required for amniocentesis. Drawbacks include problems with the quality of material extracted and sometimes ambiguous results.

Advances in specialized culturing and staining procedures are making the study of chromosome structure more and more precise. Each chromosome of the karyotype can now be identified unequivocally. Smaller and smaller variations, rearrangements, deletions, and additions in the chromosome complement can be detected by cytogeneticists.

However, any changes that can be visually detected on the level of the karyotype are very large changes involving large segments of DNA and probably a rather significantly large number of genes. The detection of biochemical disorders is a much more difficult task, which we will turn to next.

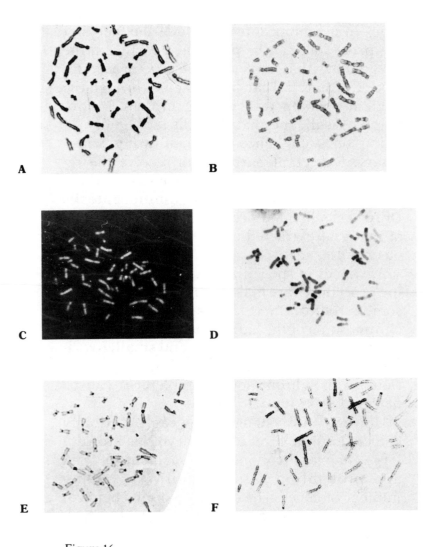

A

B

C

D

E

F

Figure 16

Staining Techniques and Chromosomes

Different types of stains and pretreatments combined with stains bring out different patterns, which can be observed in the chromosomes. These patterns facilitate studying the size, structure, and shape of the chromosomes. Figure 16 illustrates six of the most common types of staining.

A. Homogeneous stain. The entire chromosome takes on a darker appearance, making it more easily visible under the microscope. No details of internal structure are revealed.

B. G-Bands. A pattern of alternating dark and light bands makes the identification of individual chromosomes possible.

C. Q-Bands. The patterns revealed by this staining procedure are visible only under a special fluorescent microscope. It reveals not only the pattern of bands but also the variations in intensity or brightness that are unique to the individual and further aid in the identification of the chromosomes.

D. R-Bands. The bands produced by this procedure are the reverse of those produced by G-bands and Q-bands. Bands that appear light in G- and Q-banding appear dark in R-banding. R-banding is useful in the detection of translocations.

E. C-bands. C-banding, discussed in Figure 15, produces darkly stained areas in the centromeres of all chromosomes, except the Y chromosome, and variable regions of the No. 1, 9, and 16 chromosomes. It is used in the analysis of translocations and abnormalities of the No. 1, 9, and 16 chromosomes.

F. NOR-bands. This silver staining technique is used in the identification of small chromosomes.

Each staining technique may be used to reveal some specific aspect of chromosome structure. Not every technique will be necessary or useful in every case of genetic evaluation. However, at least one complete banding technique (G, Q, or R) should be used to analyze every patient.

THE TOOLS OF BIOCHEMICAL EVALUATION

Biochemical evaluation of genetic disorders is different from the analysis of chromosomal abnormalities described above. A chromosomal abnormality will be found in any cell nucleus. It doesn't matter which chromosome is involved; essentially the same test is always performed to study the chromosomes. There is no such thing as a generally applicable test for biochemical evaluation. The key feature of biochemical evaluation can be summed up in the word "specificity." No one test can indicate that *something* is wrong *somewhere* in the multitude of protein and enzyme systems in the body. The tests used in biochemical evaluation are designed for each specific disease. If the clinical examination of the patient suggests a *particular* disease, tests are undertaken to confirm or deny the diagnosis. Prenatal diagnosis of a specific biochemical disorder would be undertaken on a sample of fetal cells only if there was a family history of the disease or if the screening tests or the birth of a previous child in the family with the disease suggested that the parents were carriers of the disease.

To go into the details of the hundred or so diseases that are the subject of biochemical evaluation would be far too technical for the scope of this book. However, some general description of the kinds of measurement used in these tests is certainly in order.

A normally functioning enzyme assists in the conversion of a specific substrate into a specific product, as we have described earlier. Under controlled laboratory conditions (with proper temperature, pH, concentration, and so forth) normal cellular extracts from a patient will convert an appropriate substrate to which it is exposed into the appropriate product at a steady rate. This is so because it has a normally functioning enzyme. However, if something is wrong with the enzyme, the conversion process will be affected. If the cells have less than the normal amount of the enzyme, or if the enzyme is in some way defective, the conversion of the substrate into the product will take place at a slower rate than normal. If the enzyme is missing, the conversion will not occur. In some biochemical disorders, it is possible to gauge this conversion process accurately by quantitatively measuring either the disappearance of the substrate or the appearance of the product under controlled conditions. In this way, defective enzyme activity, reduced enzyme activity, or the absence of the enzyme can be detected.

Sometimes the presence or absence of an enzyme can be detected by its physical and chemical properties as a molecule rather than by its activity as in the tests we have just discussed.

The size, structure, and atomic makeup of a molecule give that molecule certain solubility (ability to be dissolved) and electrical characteristics. A procedure known as chromatography uses differences in solubility to separate a mixture of different molecules. A procedure known as electrophoresis uses differences in the response to an electrical field to separate molecules. Both procedures help to determine the presence or absence of the enzyme in question.

Sometimes both procedures can be used together to produce "fingerprints" of a cell extract or a digested protein. If a protein is missing from a cellular extract, its normal spot in the fingerprint would be missing. An altered protein or protein component may have different chemical or physical properties than its normal counterpart and therefore would produce an altered fingerprint.

Sometimes altered biochemical functioning produces visible changes in the cell, or changes that can, with proper laboratory preparation, become visible under the microscope. Certain cells may experience an abnormal accumulation or storage of metabolic products. Some body tissues may display abnormal shape and structure related to the genetic disease. Some biochemical disorders cause changes in the cell surface, and these changes can be made visible by special staining techniques. Radioactive tracers can be introduced into sample cells in the laboratory under controlled circumstances and be used to measure enzyme activity.

The cells used in biochemical tests depend on how the gene involved normally expresses itself. Sometimes a blood sample is the best source of test material, but different tests will be reliable with blood serum, others with red blood cells, and still others with white blood cells. Sometimes tissue from a specific organ is needed—liver, muscle, or skin, for example. Sometimes the gene product is found in body fluids such as tears.

For prenatal diagnosis of a biochemical disorder, sometimes a cell-free sample of amniotic fluid provides the most reliable test material. In other cases, cells floating in the amniotic fluid are best. Sometimes these cells must be cultured in the laboratory first to provide the most reliable results. Occasionally a direct sampling of fetal blood, skin, or other tissue is required. A modification of the fetoscopy procedure has made such direct sampling feasible.

Because enzyme activity is sensitive to changes in environmental conditions such as pH, temperature, incubation time, and concentration, careful controls are always required in biochemical evaluation. A normal control test must be performed at the same time to ensure accuracy. In prenatal diagnosis even more complications must be taken into account. The biochemist must know the fetus's age at the time of the test and how the cells have been handled and cultured before he or she makes a comparison with normal enzyme levels.

To sum up, because genetic diseases are so varied, the techniques for detecting them are likewise quite diverse. Some disorders are caused by visible chromosomal imbalances that are detected through the use of karyotypes. Some disorders originate with metabolic disturbances that are detected through biochemical analyses. Still other genetic diseases display developmental patterns (such as abnormal bone structure or skin) that make the disease visually identifiable prenatally through the use of ultrasound, X-ray, or fetoscopy.

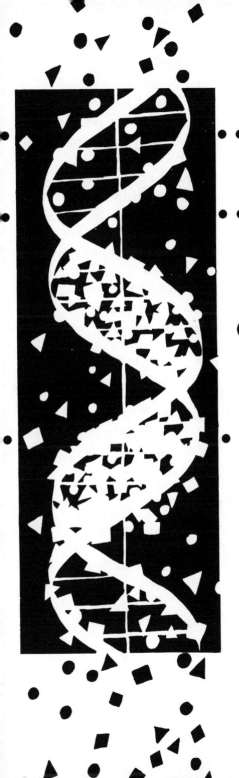

5

The Diagnosis of Genetic Disease

In the preceding chapter we discussed some of the tools of genetic evaluation. In this chapter we will take a look at how and when a physician may use these tools to diagnose genetic disease.

It is not necessary, desirable, or practical to use tests for genetic disease in each and every pregnancy or in the birth of every newborn child. In general, genetic evaluations are costly, time-consuming, and highly specialized. Existing laboratories simply could not begin to process the number of cases that would result from the indiscriminate application of genetic tests. Geneticists have concerned themselves with the need to devise ways to pinpoint more accurately specific groups within the general population who are at increased risk for a particular genetic disease and therefore are prime candidates for testing.

IDENTIFYING GROUPS AT RISK

Empirical observations have produced correlations that are helpful in identifying populations at risk for genetic diseases. Such subgroups have been defined by a variety of factors. In some cases the age of the pregnant woman is crucial. For example, there is a significantly increased risk of Down syndrome or other chromosomal abnormalities in the child when the mother is over thirty-seven years of age. Amniocentesis to obtain samples of fetal cell material for karyotyping is becoming a routine procedure in such cases. To be on the safe side, many physicians will advise amniocentesis for any pregnant woman over age thirty-five. Sometimes a genetic disease is clearly associated with populations of a particular ethnic background or geographic origin. For example, sickle-cell anemia is found among blacks predominantly, Tay-Sachs disease among Eastern European Jews, and thalassemia among Greeks and Italians. Screening for carrier status for the relevant disease may be suggested to members of these groups. Among newborn infants and developing children a cluster of symptoms may suggest the involvement of a chromosomal or metabolic disorder.

THE APPLICATION OF STEPWISE SCREENING TESTS

In a few cases, a simple, inexpensive screening test can be applied to the general population to find a smaller group that is at increased risk for a genetic disease. The screening test for abnormalities in the development and closure of the spinal cord (called neural tube defects) which measures increased levels of alphafeto protein (AFP) in maternal blood serum is a good example. This test was originally designed to identify possible neural tube defects in families in which at least one child has already been born with such defects as spina bifida (open spine). The test is based on a specifically observed increase in a protein (fetal in origin) in the amniotic fluid and the mother's serum due to an abnormal opening in the fetus's neural tube. The level of this protein is also related to the age of the fetus. This inexpensive test is performed on the mother's serum between the fifteenth and twentieth week of pregnancy. Because it is primarily a screening test that aids in pinpointing cases where additional diagnostic testing is required, interpretation of test results must be exceedingly careful. An elevated level of alphafeto protein does not necessarily mean the baby has a neural tube defect. In 97 percent of the cases, doctors find that the elevated protein level is due to something other than neural tube defects—a mistaken calculation of fetal age or length of the pregnancy, for example, or a multiple pregnancy.

The elevated protein level then is used, not to diagnose the presence of the disease, but to identify which patients must be tested further. The next step is to wait a week and draw another sample of the mother's serum. Often the alphafeto protein level is found to be normal in the second test. If elevated levels persist, ultrasound is used to determine the outline of the fetus. Many cases are eliminated from consideration at this stage because the physical look at the fetus shows that the date of pregnancy was in error or that a multiple pregnancy is involved. If suspicion persists, amniocentesis is performed to determine AFP levels in the amniotic fluid, and other tests are done as well.

This procedure has been extremely successful, as the record of the screening program at one of the pioneering labs in this field demonstrates. In a 1978 pilot study, the lab tested 17,700 pregnancies in an AFP-neural tube defects screening program, and 4 percent of the cases had elevated maternal serum results in two consecutive tests. This meant that 648 women were brought in for ultrasound examination. At this stage, some of the cases were eliminated because of errors in calculating fetal age or multiple pregnancies. Exactly 365 of the patients—only 2 percent of the original screening group—had amniocentesis performed. Twenty fetuses with neural tube defects were discovered. Out of the original

17,700 cases, only two instances of neural tube defects were missed. That happened because the neural tube openings in the fetuses had been closed over by skin tissue, preventing observation of elevated AFP levels in the original screening test. This testing program is a good demonstration of how scientists can identify a population in which complex, expensive testing is likely to be most fruitful.

Although this testing program was originally designed for use in families with a previous child born with neural tube defects, it is now recommended as a general screening test for all pregnancies because it is inexpensive and simple, and has a step by step procedure of increasingly complex testing that minimizes the possibility of a mistaken diagnosis.

AMNIOCENTESIS—A GENERAL TEST FOR SPECIFIC POPULATIONS

As we have mentioned, amniocentesis is an important diagnostic tool in prenatal genetic evaluation. Amniocentesis is recommended for couples who fall into one of the following categories:

- previous children with neural tube defects (for elevated AFP levels)
- advanced maternal age (because incidence of chromosome disorders increases significantly

TABLE 1 ● REASONS FOR REFERRALS FOR AMNIOCENTESIS

RELATIVE RISK	TYPE OF GENETIC EVALUATION		
	Neural Tube Defect	**Cytogenetic**	**Biochemical**
HIGH (more than 10%)	More than 2 previous children with neural tube defects	One parent known to be carrier of a balanced translocation One parent mosaic for trisomy Mother a carrier of sex-linked disorder Maternal age over 45 years	Both parents carriers of the same prenatally diagnosable metabolic disorder Mother a carrier of diagnosable sex-linked disease
MODERATE (3 to 5%)	One previous child with neural tube defect	Maternal age of 40–45 years	
LOW (Approx. 1%)		Previous child with Down Syndrome or other trisomy Maternal age of 35–40 years	

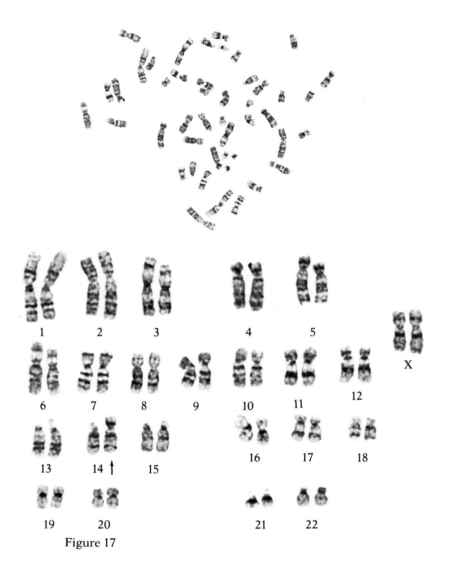

1   2   3   4   5

X

6   7   8   9   10   11   12

13   14 ↑   15   16   17   18

19   20   21   22

Figure 17

when the mother is over thirty-seven)
- one parent known to be a carrier of a balanced translocation of chromosomal material (which increases risk of chromosome imbalances in the gametes)
- a previous child with Down syndrome or other extra chromosome abnormality
- mother known to be a carrier for a sex-linked disorder (transmitted by the X-chromosome)
- both parents have been identified as carriers of a prenatally diagnosable metabolic disease.

Karyotyping of the chromosomes is done when the patient or pregnancy is at risk for chromosomal abnormalities. Karyotyping is

Translocations and Down Syndrome

The karyotype for Down syndrome does not always consist of 47 chromosomes. Sometimes the extra No. 21 chromosome is linked by translocation to another chromosome. The patient has 46 chromosomes but still has a triple dose of the No. 21 chromosome material and exhibits all the clinical symptoms of Down syndrome. In this karyotype the extra No. 21 chromosome is attached to the top of one of the No. 14 chromosomes.

When this karyotype appears in a child with Down syndrome, the parents' blood should be studied to determine if the translocation is new or inherited. Parents can carry the translocation and themselves be unaffected. With this type of translocation they would have a total of 45, not 46 chromosomes, but would have the normal, balanced dosage of all genetic material. Families with an inherited translocation would be at increased risk for producing more affected offspring.

also performed if a newborn or young child shows one of the following clinical symptoms: mental retardation; severe retardation of growth and development; congenital heart disease; a peculiar face and very short or very tall stature; an unusual palm print; abnormal development of the external genitalia; skeletal abnormalities.

GENERAL SCREENING TESTS FOR SPECIFIC BIOCHEMICAL DISORDERS

As we have pointed out before, genetic diseases are too varied for one general test to detect any and all genetic diseases. In recent years, however, some tests for specific biochemical disorders have been developed that are simple enough and inexpensive enough to be used on the general population as screening tests for those specific diseases.

DETECTING DISEASE IN THE NEWBORN INFANT

Almost every state in the United States has some kind of newborn infant screening test for a limited number of biochemical disorders. In New York, for example, babies are routinely tested at birth for eight rare but serious diseases. A small sample of the baby's blood is drawn, dried on a filter paper, and sent on to a centralized public laboratory for analysis. New York tests for these eight diseases:

- sickle-cell anemia
- phenylketonuria (PKU)
- branched-chain ketonuria—also known as maple syrup urine disease (MSUD) because of a maple syrup–like odor in the urine—caused by the body's inability to break down protein because of the lack of a necessary enzyme
- galactosemia, caused by the lack of an enzyme necessary for breaking down milk sugar
- homocystinuria, caused by a missing enzyme in the liver and sometimes resulting in mental retardation
- histidinemia, caused by a missing enzyme and sometimes resulting in mental retardation and speech defects
- adenosine deaminase deficiency, caused by a missing enzyme and sometimes resulting in susceptibility to infection
- hypothyroidism, caused by improper production of the hormone thyroxine and sometimes leading to mental and physical retardation.

These diseases are all quite rare. The most common one, sickle-cell anemia, occurs in only one of every five hundred black newborn infants. Hypothyroidism, the next most common, occurs in one of every four thousand births.

Adenosine deaminase deficiency is the least common, occurring only once in every half-million births. They are all serious diseases, but if they are detected early some can be treated and the patient's suffering reduced. The screening program now in use in New York is a significant step forward in identifying patients and families at risk for these diseases. Unfortunately these diseases represent only a very small number of the many inborn errors of metabolism in humans.

TESTING A SPECIFIC POPULATION

Other tests are available for use where an at-risk population can be defined by other criteria. A good example is Tay-Sachs disease, an extremely serious disorder generally resulting in death between the ages of three and five. Babies born with the disease appear normal at birth. The first symptoms begin to appear when the infant is between four and eight months of age. By age ten months the baby becomes apathetic, less attentive. After that, there is a progressive deterioration of development. A baby who used to be able to sit up by itself, for example, loses that ability. By eighteen months, it can no longer hold up its own head. By two years, the child is likely to have become blind and nonresponsive. This degeneration continues until death. There is no therapy for this disease. It is a tragedy for the child and for the entire family.

The cause of Tay-Sachs disease has been traced to the buildup of certain abnormal intermediate cell by-products as a result of improper enzyme activity. It is inherited as a recessive trait and is most likely to be found among Jewish people whose ancestors came from Lithuania, a country in Eastern Europe. Members of this population are ten times more likely to be carriers of the recessive gene causing this disease than are members of the general population. They are a hundred times more likely to bear children who will be stricken with the disease.

A rapid, inexpensive screening test has been devised to detect carrier status in members of the at-risk population (Eastern European Jews and their descendants) and has been used quite successfully. As knowledge of the availability of this test has become more widely known in the Jewish community, an increasing number of young Jewish couples have sought out the screening test. The identification of carriers of the disease permits physicians to monitor the pregnancies more closely and conduct prenatal tests on the fetuses. Rather than giving birth to a baby afflicted with this terrible disease and doomed to an agonizing life and early death, parents may choose a therapeutic abortion and try again for a healthy baby. This procedure has resulted in a 65 to 85 percent reduction in the birth of Tay-Sachs children in the Jewish population.

To summarize, increasing the accuracy of their diagnostic ability is a prime concern for geneticists. They are also concerned about devising improved and reliable ways to identify individuals, and groups of individuals, for whom genetic testing and evaluation are appropriate. These methods take into account certain empirical observations (clinical symptoms, maternal age, family history) and the results of inexpensive screening tests applied to large sections of the community. The search for inexpensive, effective, increasingly sophisticated screening procedures continues all the time.

6

Cancer
and
Genetics

Probably no disease arouses as much fear and concern in our society as cancer does. One person in four will develop cancer in his or her lifetime. Virtually everyone knows someone who has died of the disease. Public concern is widespread. About a decade ago, amid much hoopla, the Nixon administration announced a "war" on cancer. Millions were earmarked for research. Every day the media seem to carry a hopeful story about a medical breakthrough, but these stories always seem to fade. There are more than one hundred different cancers. All are characterized by a breakdown in the body's control over its processes, and by a proliferation of cancerous cells, which thrive at the expense of other cells and of the body as a whole. But as yet, scientists are not really sure what causes cancer or how to cure it.

Is cancer on the increase in modern society? This question is difficult to answer. Thanks to advances in medicine, improved living conditions, and better nutrition, people live longer today than in previous periods of human history. People tend to survive diseases that in the past would have proved fatal. As a consequence, it may just be that people are now surviving long enough to succumb to cancer.

Another characteristic of modern life may be a significant contributor to the high rate of cancer today. Environmental factors that never existed before interact in a dynamic way with the genetic makeup of individuals and foster the development of cancer. These dangerous environmental factors seem to increase all the time. Much is already known about the dangerously disruptive effects of X-rays, which may be related to cancer. Controversy rages over the potential dangers of such sources of radiation as nuclear testing, nuclear power plants, and nuclear waste disposal. Controversy is just beginning over the possible effects of radiation emitted by computer display terminals. Atmospheric pollutants and chemicals used in the work place and at home may also be related to the development of cancers in some patients who are genetically predisposed to the disease.

It is very difficult to determine the impact of environmental substances on the incidence of cancer. Sometimes it takes decades for the cancer-contributing effects to become apparent. A notable example of this is the case of the shipyard workers exposed to asbestos in the construction of naval warships during World War II. Little was known about the cancer-related hazards of asbestos exposure until thirty years later when these shipyard workers began exhibiting symptoms.

THE RELATIONSHIP BETWEEN GENETICS AND CANCER

A number of questions arise about the relationship between cancer and genetics. Can cancer be inherited? Can the insults to our biological system stemming from the environment cause cancer? Are some people more likely to get cancer because of their genetic makeup? Can genetics serve as a tool to identify the most harmful chemicals and substances before they enter the marketplace and the food chain?

The exact relationship between genetics and cancer is unclear. The control exerted by the genetic code in maintaining normal health functions in a very complex manner. This control is exerted on each cell as well as on the entire organism. It has to be integrated with the internal environment within the organism and the external environment in which the organism lives.

Cancer is characterized by a rampant proliferation of abnormal cells at the expense of the rest of the body, and this proliferation can occur only if the normal control mechanisms have broken down. The first breakdown apparently occurs in the cancer cell itself. For the disease to establish itself, a breakdown also seems to be necessary in the body's ability to halt or contain the growth of these abnormal cancerous cells.

Considerable evidence indicates that cancer cells are genetically different from normal cells of the patient in which they grow. The first changes may be invisible point mutations affecting a single gene. Recent research suggests that human beings may have as few as a dozen or so major "cancer genes." When functioning normally, these genes serve as a control mechanism, keeping the body in balance. When altered, they may become potent *decontrol* mechanisms, allowing abnormal cells to outgrow normal cells. Since more than a hundred different forms of cancer apparently can be triggered by the action of these few cancer genes, we must conclude that these genes are very powerful and fundamental control mechanisms. The nature of these genes and the way they function remains for researchers to discover.

Although the first genetic changes in cancer cells occur on the invisible level of gene mutations, the analysis of animal and human tumors indicates that at some point the changes become visible on the level of the chromosomes. Cancer cells begin to display abnormalities in mitotic cell division, reflect-

The Development of Cancer

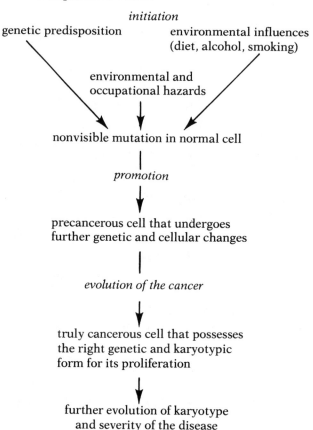

Figure 18

ing metabolic disturbances within the cell. Chromosomes fail to separate properly during cell division. This results in cells with abnormal chromosome numbers. Some cancer cells may have extra chromosomes. Some may have lost chromosomes. Broken and reattached chromosomes may result in cells with structurally abnormal chromosomes. Such chromosomal abnormalities cause an imbalance in the genetic information and may help the cell complete its transformation to malignancy.

Does the chromosomal change we have described cause the cancer, or does the cancer cause the chromosome change? The precise answer to this question is still a mystery. It may prove to be a little of both. In a normal state the body is not tolerant of extremely abnormal chromosome arrangements and number. Normally cells missing chromosomes do not survive; they die out. There are only three types of autosomal trisomies (condition where there are three of one of the chromosomes instead of the normal pair) are known to be compatible with the fetus surviving till birth. But the cancerous states seem very tolerant of abnormal chromosome number and structure. Karyotypes of human cancer tumors have demonstrated the existence of cancer cells ranging from the normal complement of forty-six chromosomes up to more than a thousand chromosomes! In some cases scientists were able to prove that the abnormal cells had all descended from a single, original cancer cell. In other cases evidence indicated that wide proliferation of varied ancestor cells was involved.

Research may someday reveal that a specific chromosome change is crucial for certain forms of cancer or that, in other cases, the ability of the disease to produce cells with widely divergent karyotypes may provide a pool from which cells may be drawn with a selective growth advantage at some point in the evolution of the disease. But all of this is still at the speculative level. Much research remains to be done.

However, it is now an accepted fact that chromosomal abnormalities are significant in cancer, either as a cause or as an effect. Certain chromosomal abnormalities appear to be linked to a predisposition to cancer. For example, Down syndrome, which is caused by an extra No. 21 chromosome, increases the risk of leukemia (cancer of the blood). Fanconi's anemia and Bloom syndrome, which involve chromosome instability and increased likelihood of chromosome breakage, predispose an individual patient to cancer.

Even though the causal relationship between cancer and chromosomal abnormalities is still largely a mystery, physicians are able to use the information already at their disposal as a tool in diagnosing and treating certain cancer patients. In some cases, the presence of a particular chromosome pattern may help doctors distinguish a cancerous from a noncancerous illness. In other cases, the chromosome pattern may help them distinguish an acute form (in which the disease is progressing at rapid pace) from a chronic form (in which the disease is progressing at a much slower pace). In still other cases, the chromosome pattern allows doctors to identify the onset of a critical stage in the development of the disease. This information may influence the choice of treatment or may be used to monitor the effectiveness of the treatment. It can also be used to determine whether the disease has entered into a period of remission, or a dormant stage, in which the patient's symptoms abate.

The treatment of chronic myelogenous leukemia is a good example of how chromosome examination can be used in monitoring cancer. Scientists have observed a characteristic "marker" chromosome, called the Philadelphia chromosome, which is present in approximately 85 to 90 percent of all chronic myelogenous leukemia patients. Research points to a strong relationship between this chromosome change and the disease itself. Part of the No. 22 chromosome is lost or relocated to another chromosome, usually the No. 9. Apparently all the cancerous cells derive from a single cell with this chromosomal rearrangement. Remission of the disease is detected by the reappearance of chromosomally normal cells. The crisis stage is detected by an increase in chromosomal abnormalities. By analyzing the chromosomes along with other clinical evidence, physicians can more accurately de-

Karyotype of Leukemia Patient with Philadelphia Marker

Cells from the bone marrow of patients with chronic myelogenous leukemia possess a particular abnormal karyotype in about 85 percent of all cases. The rearrangement involves a transfer of a portion of a No. 22 chromosome to the bottom of a No. 9 chromosome (see arrows in photo). The presence of this karyotype may be of help in the diagnosis, treatment, and monitoring of the disease. This characteristic rearrangement is known as the Philadelphia marker.

Karyotypic abnormalities have been observed in a number of other leukemias, and karyotyping has become an increasingly important diagnostic tool for hematologists.

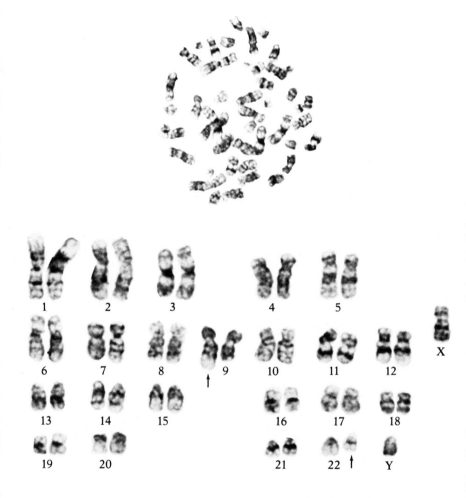

Figure 19

termine what stage of the disease the patient is experiencing, and provide appropriate treatment.

GENETIC SUSCEPTIBILITY TO CANCER

Despite the many mysteries about the relationship between cancer and genetics, it does seem that genetics influences susceptibility to cancer and the way in which the disease progresses.

Laboratory research has clearly proven that certain genetically different strains of experiment animals exhibit different degrees of susceptibility to cancer, both to cancers caused by spontaneous formation and to cancers caused by exposure to cancer-inducing substances in the environment. Among human beings, family histories show that some families tend to have a higher than average incidence of particular forms of cancer. Whether this is the result of chance, some common environmental cause, or a genetic predisposition is unclear.

Certain types of genetic disruption are also linked to an increased disposition toward cancer. We have already mentioned the activity of the "cancer genes." Other dominant and recessive genes cause various other diseases, but they also carry along with them an increased likelihood of cancer. A disruption of the body's immune system, caused by genetic change, may ultimately contribute to cancer because of the body's diminished capacity to combat the disease. A dominant gene that disturbs the growth pattern in certain body tissues may lead to malignancies. Recessive genes may cause an increase in spontaneous chromosome damage, or an increased susceptibility to environmental insults that are linked to a higher than average cancer incidence.

To sum up, a cancerous cell may develop and grow in a person who has a predisposition to cancer, even in a relatively healthful environment. Under the same conditions, a person *without* a predisposition to cancer will probably not develop the disease. In an unhealthful environment, in which individuals are subjected to abnormally high exposure to cancer-inducing substances, even a person who is not genetically predisposed to cancer may develop the disease. Genetic research is concerned not only with identifying those individuals and groups who are susceptible to cancer, but also with identifying those environmental substances that increase the rate of genetic mutation to abnormally high levels, contribute to the development of cancer, or cause birth defects. The identification of such potentially deadly substances before they become an integral part of our normal environment in modern society and seriously endanger public health is a crucial task. This is the subject of our next chapter.

7

Pollution
and
Genetics

In the past decade we have become increasingly aware of the need to protect ourselves against the menace of environmental hazards. The broad-ranging impact environmental insults can have on our finely tuned biological systems has been clearly recognized.

- In the first decade of the 1900s private industries used the Love Canal area near Buffalo, New York, as a dumping site for over 200,000 tons of chemical waste. In the late 1940s the federal government may have dumped radioactive waste materials there. A few years later a housing development was built at the site. Twenty-five years later, Love Canal residents were up in arms because of abnormally high rates of cancer, birth defects, miscarriages, and liver, kidney, and respiratory diseases in their neighborhood. The increase in disease was attributed to their constant exposure to the festering pollution hidden below their homes.
- During World War II thousands of American workers labored long and hard in shipyards throughout the country. They were exposed to the asbestos that was used in the construction of the ships. Thirty to forty years later these workers suffer an abnormally high cancer rate. Johns Manville, a corporation that manufactured asbestos, recently declared bankruptcy, in part because of billions of dollars in lawsuits filed against the company by affected workers and their families.
- In the early 1950s the United States military conducted nuclear weapons tests at sites in isolated

areas of the Nevada desert. At the time, the government assured residents in areas of Nevada and Utah which were downwind of the blast sites that they need fear no health risks because of the tests. Believing what their government told them, entire families would stand outside their homes and gaze at clouds of nuclear fallout passing overhead. Today lawsuits are being tried in the courts in behalf of affected people who want to hold the American government liable for the increased cancer they suffered.

- In the 1950s an antinausea drug known as DES was prescribed for many pregnant women. Today the daughters of these women suffer a greatly increased rate of uterine cancer. Recent evidence indicates an increased rate of testicular cancer for sons of women who took DES.

- The biggest liability judgment rendered against a private company in an environmental pollution case in recent years involved the dumping of mercury waste into the sea off the Japanese coast. The mercury waste was soon incorporated into the food chain. It was ingested by fish in the area and became concentrated in the organs of the fish. These fish were a major source of protein for the local population in a nearby coastal village. Village fishermen caught the fish that had injested the mercury. The villagers ate the fish, and the mercury accumulated in their body tissue. The mercury could not be cleansed or eliminated. The accumulation of this toxic material in the bodies of the villagers led to a deterioration in health. The more mercury the individual accumulated, the worse the illness became. Tremendous pain and suffering ensued, and no cure was possible. Because Japan is an island nation, dependent on the sea as a source of food supply, Japanese public opinion was aroused and today Japan has strict laws governing the dumping of waste materials.

What is the relationship of genetics to this serious issue of pollution? As we have seen, the genetic program operates every moment of our lives. Pollutants represent a disruption of the normal environment in which the genetic program was designed to function through evolution over millions of years. Pollutants impinge on the normal functioning of the program. They can be lethal, making it impossible for the genetic program to be carried out, making life impossible. They can be distorting, robbing the individual of normal health. Or they can cause genetic disorders that can be passed on to the next generation. Pollutants don't necessarily destroy or alter genes; they can disrupt or frustrate the normal implementation of the instructions coded in the DNA. An estimated 90 percent of all malignant diseases may be influenced by some sort of environmental agent.

Geneticists have concerned themselves with helping to devise ways to detect substances that might be irritants, teratogens (causing birth defects), mutagens (causing mutations), or carcinogens (causing cancer).

TESTING NEW SUBSTANCES IN THE ENVIRONMENT

Huge numbers of new chemicals and industrial by-products are introduced into the environment of any modern technological society. Most new industrial chemicals, pesticides, drugs, food additives, and cosmetic components introduced each year are tested to determine if exposure to them can cause death. Obviously it's important to know whether a new chemical will kill people or not before allowing it to be put on the market. But this is only the most extreme possibility in a broad spectrum of potentially harmful effects. Additional testing is required to detect various nonlethal effects, including the impairment of health or an increase in the incidence of cancer or birth defects. Unfortunately such testing is not routinely performed on all new chemicals we are exposed to.

In the best of all possible worlds it would probably be preferable to test everything. Why risk making a mistake and allowing a harmful substance into the environment? But we don't live in such a world today. There is considerable resistance to general testing of all new chemical substances. Business, government, and medical officials opposed to such testing express concern about the impact of long delays while testing goes on, about the cost involved, and about the relative balance between costs and benefits.

Certain criteria, then, have to be used to decide which new chemicals should be tested more thoroughly than others. Obviously the first consideration is how dangerous the chemical is suspected of being. If a new chemical has certain effects already proven dangerous, further testing is clearly appropriate. If the chemical is a variant of another substance already known to be hazardous, additional testing would likewise be necessary. Although industry sometimes resists testing such chemicals—either because testing would be costly or because the chemical is necessary to industrial processes regardless of risk—the general population for the most part sees the importance of thoroughly testing such dangerous substances.

A less obvious consideration is the number of people who will be exposed to the substance. Suppose that a new chemical is thought to have only a moderate risk of being harmful, but its anticipated uses in industry would mean that a large number of people would be exposed to it. Under these circumstances this moderate-risk, high-exposure chemical would be a prime candidate for additional testing.

Scientists must also take into account what the body is likely to do with the chemical after ingesting or absorbing it. The chemical itself is only part of the consideration. The metabolic system of the body alters chemicals. Although the original chemical may not be toxic to the body, one of the metabolic products might be, and this must be known in order to determine the potential hazards associated with the substance.

The tests themselves have to be carefully designed so that they will detect all hazards likely to affect human beings. Otherwise, hazardous materials will slip through, and we may not learn about the dangers involved until decades later when the effects become observable in human beings. The likelihood of cancer among shipyard workers exposed to asbestos forty years ago is a prime example of such a tragedy. To be of any value, the testing programs for new chemicals must be made on experimental organisms that use the substance in a manner parallel to the way in which human beings would use it. This is the only way to get an idea of the likely impact of the chemical on human beings without testing it on them, which is morally and ethically out of the question. The tests must be inexpensive enough and rapid enough to be usable by industry, and they must be sensitive enough to detect all hazards without giving an inordinate number of false results. These requirements mean much effort has to go into designing testing programs.

The simplest tests usually involve the application of the test chemical to the skin of the experimental animal. In the case of cosmetics, the test chemical is sprayed in the eyes of the experimental animal. The animal is then studied for irritation or allergic reactions. In studies documenting the hazards of cigarette smoking, laboratory animals inhale smoke to the same degree as human smokers would over an extended period. Then a pathological study is done to determine the development of disease in the animals' lungs. These findings are then correlated with statistics available on the incidence of lung cancer among human smokers.

TERATOGENS

Certain chemical agents act directly on the developmental process and are capable of causing abnormalities in unborn children. These substances are called teratogens. They act on the fetus as it is still developing within the usually safe and sheltered environment of the mother's womb. Teratogens either travel through the mother's system to the fetus or alter the mother's system in a manner adversely affecting the baby.

Teratogens are highly specific in the way they function. We may not know exactly how a teratogen causes an abnormality in the fetus, but we do know that there is usually a precise, critical time in the developmental process when it does its damage to the baby. We also know that each teratogen affects a specific organ or group of organs. The degree of impact of the teratogen is directly related to the point in the differentiation process at which the teratogen is introduced.

The embryo is especially vulnerable to teratogens in the early stages of pregnancy. Problems caused by active teratogens during the first two weeks after fertilization generally result in early prenatal death and spontaneous abortion. From the fifteenth to the sixtieth day of pregnancy, teratogens may still cause death but are more likely to cause physical abnormalities. The earlier in this period exposure to the teratogen occurs the more severe the deformity or abnormality is likely to be. Later exposure, when tissue differentiation has progressed further, is likely to result in minor abnormalities.

Known teratogens include X-rays, German measles virus (rubella), smoking, alcohol, certain medications (thalidomide and DES, for example), and certain food additives.

Radiation from X-rays can damage the baby's central nervous system and eyes and can cause mental retardation. Rubella can cause cataracts, deafness, and ear defects. Certain hormone treatments can cause masculinization of baby girls (a distortion of female genitalia). Certain antitumor drugs may cause skeletal and central nervous system defects and stunted growth. Tetracycline, an antibiotic drug, may cause tooth defects during the first six months of pregnancy. Taken in extremely large doses, tetracycline may cause cataracts. Smoking during pregnancy cuts the blood supply to the uterus, which decreases the oxygen and nutrient supply to the fetus. This decrease can mean a slowed growth rate and defective mental development. Mothers who smoke twenty cigarettes a day are twice as likely to have a premature delivery as mothers who are nonsmokers. Chronic alcoholics run the risk of bearing children who suffer from growth deficiency and mental retardation.

Their babies also suffer a higher incidence of birth defects of the joints and heart disease.

The effects of most teratogens can be seen at birth, as birth defects, but the results of others don't appear until years later. For example, the increased incidence of uterine cancer among the daughters of women treated during pregnancy with the antinausea drug, DES, is not showing up until the daughters reach their twenties.

Testing substances for possible teratogenic effects before they are put on the market is an extremely serious matter and must be carefully done. Tests must be correlated with the known action of teratogens, and they must be made on laboratory animals whose metabolic system closely parallels that of the human. Environmental substances to which pregnant women are likely to be exposed must be tested. Since teratogens have an impact on the developing fetus, tests must be conducted on pregnant laboratory animals in a manner simulating the way in which human exposure is likely to occur (inhalation, skin contact, injection, or ingestion).

The level of exposure to the teratogen has to be high enough to trigger an effect, and the timing of exposure must be appropriate. Typically this means exposure early in pregnancy, when the embryo is most sensitive to teratogens. Researchers keep track of the rate of fetal death and abnormal development of the experimental animals so that a judgment can be made as to whether the environmental agent is causing abnormalities beyond what would normally occur by chance. However, this type of testing is inadequate to detect teratogens with delayed effects, such as DES. In such cases testing must follow laboratory animals beyond birth into the next generation.

Because of the tremendous number of substances introduced into the environment annually, it is perhaps inevitable that some teratogens slip through the safety net of the testing programs and come to attention only after some tragedy. Population studies and detailed investigations of fetal deaths, premature births, low birth weight of newborn babies, and declining chances for survival often reveal hints about what new substances may be dangerous and ought to be studied further. Educational programs can alert pregnant women about the need to maintain a proper diet and avoid dangerous substances during pregnancy. If need be, such substances can be banned or exposure to them minimized.

MUTAGENS

Some environmental substances can cause alterations in the genetic code, or mutations. These substances are called mutagens. Mutations aren't always bad. Indeed spontaneous mutations are the source of genetic variability and the basis of evolutionary change. The rich variety of life on earth stems from mutations. Why, then, are we so concerned about the action of mutagenic substances? The answer is that these substances have unnaturally and dramatically increased the rate of mutation at the same time that advances in medical science have decreased the influence of natural selection.

Mutagenic substances don't always cause mutations. They may merely increase the rate of mutations. The human system has built-in safeguards against mutagenic insults from the environment. DNA-synthesizing enzymes are designed to reject certain types of error out of hand, unless of course the action of the enzymes is affected by the mutagenic agents. Other enzyme systems can repair mutations in synthesized DNA by excising the error, perhaps an incorrect base, and replacing it with the proper base. Metabolic systems in the cells and tissues may detoxify mutagens by converting them to another form. (However, this may sometimes make the problem even worse, if it results in a conversion to another mutagenic or a carcinogenic product.) The final method the human system uses to handle unfavorable mutations is natural selection, the decreased chances for survival of the affected individual.

Where mutations occur is also a factor involved in the body's ability to minimize their impact. If changes in the DNA occur in cells involved in sexual reproduction—the egg cells or the sperm cells—they may be passed along to the offspring. However, in such cases, decreased chances for survival may block the passage of the altered DNA to the next generation if the change is sufficiently harmful to the developing fetus. If DNA changes occur in body, or somatic, cells, they will be passed on only to cells descended from the originally altered cell within the affected individual, not to that individual's children.

The DNA change may occur on the nonvisible level of a point mutation, involving changes in base sequences, or deletions of bases, as we discussed in Chapter 3. The DNA change may also occur on the observable level, involving changes in the structure or arrangement of the chromosomes.

Mutagens appear to act randomly on the entire structure of the gene, though research with bacteria cells suggests that some sites on the gene may be more vulnerable to change than others. A mutation may occur instantaneously, such as those mutations caused by exposure to X-rays. Or a mutation may be induced by continued exposure to the mutagen over an extended period of time, suggesting either that the mutation results from a buildup of effects or that the mutation occurs through the laws of probability, with chances for mutation greatly increased because of increased exposure.

The expression of the altered DNA may occur in the next generation, or it may take several generations to show up, depending on whether the mutation is dominant or recessive change. A dominant lethal gene mutation will express itself in the death of an offspring. A rare recessive gene might take generations to express itself.

Some mutagens may also be cancer inducers (carcinogens) that will allow the uncontrolled proliferation of abnormal cells. The action of carcinogens appears to begin on the nonvisible level of mutations in highly potent oncogenes (cancer genes). Unlike the generalized action of most mutagens, there is sometimes a specific relationship between the carcinogen and the effect it produces: smoking and inhaling asbestos are related to lung cancer, radiation exposure is related to skin cancer, and so forth. Exposure tends to occur over long periods, and the expression of the carcinogenic change may take decades to be seen.

In human beings many mutations today result in disease. Mutations may be immediately harmful to health, or they may manifest themselves only over long periods of time when the individual is exposed to a particularly stressful environment.

Detection of mutagenic substances before they hurt individuals or threaten the human species on a larger scale is more and more a major concern of medical science. Some mutagenicity testing programs parallel those described for screening teratogens. However, mutagen testing is quite a complex matter. Because mutagens don't all act in the same way, a single test is not good enough to screen all possible mutagens. Rather than simply wait for suspected mutagenic agents to come to attention in the aftermath of disastrous genetic tragedies, scientists have tried to make use of their theoretical understanding of how mutagens work to devise more thorough advance-screening tests. Scientists reason that mutagens cause injury to the DNA-coded genetic program either by reacting directly with the DNA, or by interfering with the availability of components for the DNA, or by reacting with the enzymes and proteins required to assemble or repair the DNA.

Over the past decade, a battery of four tests has been devised. These tests take into account the number of possible ways that significant alterations in the genetic code can occur and how these changes may be manifested on the nonvisible level (point mutation), the visible level (chromosomes), or the level of developmental disorders. To determine the ability of chemical substances to produce nonvisible changes in DNA, the tests use bacteria as an experimental subject. To examine changes in the chromosomes, cell division is studied. To evaluate the ability of a substance to induce disastrous developmental defects, laboratory animals and their offspring are analyzed. Comparisons between observations made in the different types of tests in this battery are done to double-check on the metabolic aspects of the problem—to see any possible impact of by-products of the test substance produced in the normal course of the body's metabolic functioning.

This battery of tests can be applied simul-

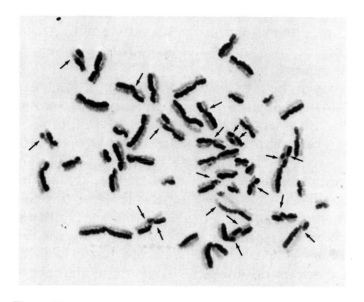

Figure 20

Sister Chromatid Exchange

Most chromosome breaks are repaired by the cell and go undetected by conventional staining techniques. By growing cells in a special growth medium and using special staining procedures, one arm of each duplicated chromosome appears lighter than the other. This makes it possible to see some evidence of breaks and reattachments involving an exchange of material between parts of the duplicated chromosomes (called sister chromatid exchange). The arrows in the figure indicate where such exchanges have occurred. The number of sister chromatid exchanges (SCEs) can be used as a measure of damage done by agents to which the individual or the cells have been exposed.

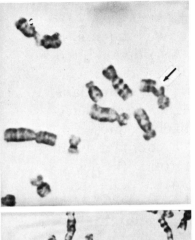

A

Figure 21
Chromosome Breakage and Mutagens and Teratogens

Chromosome breakage may be used as a measure of the damage-causing potential of agents being tested for mutagenicity and teratogenicity. In this figure, **A** represents a break in one of the duplicated chromosome pairs (chromatid), **B** represents a chromosome break and gap (see arrows), and **C** shows major breaks and rearrangements of the chromosomes due to radiation exposure.

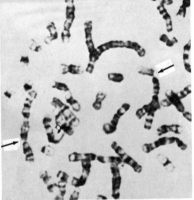

B

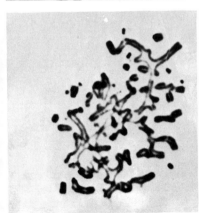

C

taneously or in sequence and is capable of yielding good information. A compound producing negative results in all four tests is considered likely to be nonmutagenic to humans. A mutagenic compound might escape detection in one test, but would likely be picked up in another. Once detected, a compound can then be further tested to determine the degree of its mutagenicity and the amount of danger it poses. Determinations can then be made about restricting its use or banning it entirely if it's extremely dangerous.

Genetic Engineering: From Modifying the Environment to Manipulating the Genetic Code

"The plain fact is that genetic engineering has the capacity to change our society," Senator Edward M. Kennedy has said. "How do we want it changed? What uses can we make of this knowledge? What degree of change is desirable, and at what rate? What kind of society do we want to become?"

Perhaps no scientific issue in recent years has been more controversial than genetic engineering. This emotionally explosive issue triggers great fears, high expectations, and confusion—all at the same time. Newspaper reporters and TV commentators conjure up terrifying images of a bleak future like that Aldous Huxley pictured in his novel *Brave New World*, on the one hand. They also provide inflated promises of wondrous medical cures, on the other hand.

It's not just the media that has plunged into the debate. Pope John Paul II a few years ago warned that genetic experiments constitute a threat to "man's right to life" and "functional integrity." The mayor of Cambridge, Massachusetts, the home of such prestigious institutions as Harvard University and Massachusetts Institute of Technology, voiced fears that genetic engineering research might lead to the release of "Frankenstein" monsters into the community. Scientists themselves have raised crucial questions about safety and morality and ethics involved in genetic research. Nobel Laureate George Wald, for example, has said that genetic engineering is the "largest ethical problem science has ever had to face."

In this chapter we will attempt to examine both the promise and the risks of genetic engineering, and to put the controversy into perspective.

DEMYSTIFYING THE PROBLEM

The phrase "genetic engineering" has a certain high-tech quality to it, a futuristic sound. In actuality, however, the human race has practiced genetic engineering for thousands of years. Any attempt to enhance artificially the survivability of a variety of plant or animal life or to select for or against a particular type through selective reproductive choices constitutes genetic engineering. Indeed, one prominent observer has argued that the Stone Age was "the finest hour" of genetic engineering, because it was then that humanity made the crucial choices about which crop plants to cultivate. (This constituted the beginning of agriculture and opened the possibility for an end to a nomadic existence in search of food and the foundation of civilization as we have come to know it.)

Practically all forms of medical intervention could also qualify as genetic engineering, in the sense that they correct various malfunctions stemming ultimately from the genetic program coded in the DNA. Women who used to die in childbirth because they inherited too narrow a pelvic bone structure were saved by the invention of the forceps, which is used by physicians to pull the baby through the birth canal, or by cesarean section—removing the baby from the uterus surgically. Hormone treatments, antibiotics, life-sustaining equipment, and organ transplants are other examples of medical procedures to correct biological malfunctions and improve chances for survival.

As the technology involved in these medical procedures has advanced over the years, new ethical and moral issues have been raised. When does life end? When should life-sustaining equipment be turned off? The ability prenatally to detect birth defects and the option of a therapeutic abortion in such cases raises moral and religious questions: which defects are so serious that parents should seek an abortion, and which are not?

But while these issues are serious, most people have not had too much difficulty accepting these types of genetic engineering as examples of beneficial medical progress. Such procedures have been historically consistent with humanity's continued attempts to modify the environment to enhance the chances for survival. The controversy has erupted over very recent breakthroughs in molecular genetics, which open up the possibility of manipulating DNA and the genetic code for the very first time in human history.

TINKERING WITH THE GENETIC CODE

The realm of recombinant DNA, an area of molecular genetics, is both fascinating and frightening to many people. Recombinant DNA deals with the dissection and reassembling of the genetic code. Using advanced techniques, scientists can actually take DNA from one type of organism and splice it onto the DNA from another, creating a new combination of genetic material, creating a new living molecule that may never have existed before.

Researchers have isolated a number of enzymes that permit this type of manipulation of DNA molecules. Some of these enzymes have the ability to "nick" the DNA strand at specific points along the chain, thereby breaking the long molecule into smaller but reproducible pieces. Different types of these "restriction" enzymes make nicks in different locations on the chain and produce different types of DNA fragments. Still other enzymes have been isolated that can be used to copy DNA fragments, or synthesize artificial DNA chains, or join DNA fragments together under specific conditions.

Concentrating their research on cultured cells in the laboratory, scientists have successfully extracted the entire DNA complement of cell nuclei. They have been able to break apart the DNA molecules and isolate fragments, using the restriction enzymes to nick or cut DNA chains at specific points along their lengths, probably, scientists believe, at specific base sequences. Researchers have even been able to identify and characterize some of the DNA fragments, based on a variety of techniques using indirect observations and judgments made according to the gene product produced. This information has served as the basis for the compilation of elaborate "gene libraries" of DNA containing single genes or clusters of genes from a variety of organisms. These libraries can then be drawn upon for studying gene regulation and development and for locating the precise gene sites responsible for different gene products.

Isolating a single gene or specific gene is an exceedingly difficult process. It is impossible to see a single gene under the microscope, just as it is impossible, for instance, to see a single atom of gold. In order to experiment with or manipulate a specific gene or gene segment, the scientist needs thousands and thousands of copies of that strand of DNA to work with.

One way that significant and usable amounts of specific DNA fragments have been obtained is by attaching the desired DNA fragment to the DNA of a virus or plasmid (a short length of DNA found in bacteria), which is then introduced into a host cell. In this way, the DNA fragment can be cloned or amplified, perhaps as much as 10,000 to 100,000 times.

A spinoff of this technique of transplanting DNA fragments into host cells and amplifying them thousands of times is the possibility of producing large quantities of the cell product coded for by the DNA fragment. The tremendously increased quantity of the DNA fragment would theoretically produce a correspondingly great quantity of the cell product involved. This procedure opens up the possibility of actually turning a single cell into a living factory, turning out a desired biological product. This possibility has spurred the formation of private companies specializing in recombinant DNA research and development. These companies hope to reap huge profits from the mass production of human biological products such as insulin. Until now, diabetes patients requiring insulin treatments have had to use insulin derived from pigs. The use of any animal-derived medication entails certain health risks. It is possible that the patient's immune system might produce antibodies to combat the pig-derived insulin. If these potential complictions could be avoided by the use of insulin derived from human cells, it would be an important medical breakthrough.

The ability to insert genes into a cell and have them express themselves opens up other possible medical applications for DNA research. It is theoretically possible that this technique could be used to treat and eliminate certain genetic diseases prenatally. A normally functioning DNA sequence could be inserted into the fertilized egg of a mother known to carry two deleterious versions of the gene in question. By introducing the normal gene into the fertilized egg, the genetic program could be corrected, or at least compensated for.

The potential uses of recombinant DNA we have described thus far represent the positive side of the genetic engineering controversy. If this were the whole story, it would be difficult to imagine what the furor is all about. What dangers are inherent in manipulating the genetic code and the biological regulatory mechanism?

THE HAZARDS OF RECOMBINANT DNA

The ability to manipulate the genetic code was a dramatic scientific development; one scientist has called it the "last scientific revolution." Almost as soon as research had begun, however, noted experts in the field itself began to warn of potential dangers. In 1974 Paul Berg and a group of other distinguished scientists, published a document in the July 24 issue of *Science*. They called on their colleagues throughout the world to postpone three types of potentially dangerous recombinant DNA experiments until an international conference could be convened to discuss the issues and initiate the process of drawing up research guidelines. They also raised serious questions about whether recombinant DNA experiments should be performed at all, considering that so little is known about the properties and characteristics of the new molecules being created.

Generally, scientists oppose any attempt to interfere with or restrict their research. They regard it as a basic right of academic freedom to pursue research wherever it may lead. Yet, the issues raised in the "Berg Letter" were so crucial and so fundamental that the voluntary moratorium was accepted by scientists throughout the world. The international conference known as the Asimolar Conference met in February 1975 in California. After considerable debate on issues of safety, the properties of the new molecules, academic freedom, social policy, and legal liability, the scientists agreed to resume research, but also to establish guidelines. They even agreed that certain experiments were potentially so dangerous that they ought not to be performed. Despite this unprecedented agreement to proceed cautiously and to restrict research voluntarily, the controversy over recombinant DNA research has continued.

What is the furor all about? What issues are at stake? The questions raised about recombinant DNA research range from scientific and technical considerations to moral, ethical, and political issues.

One of the first things to consider is the lack of exactitude involved in the fragment of DNA researchers work with. The DNA molecules are so tiny they cannot be seen under the microscope and are difficult to characterize accurately. Researchers don't really know for sure what they are working with. They can characterize the fragments by their size, by the enzymes used to generate them, and sometimes by the cell products produced. But in most cases they have no idea whether they are dealing with a cluster of genes, a single gene, or a part of a single gene. Scientists don't really know what consequences might result from taking a gene out of its normal context. Genes may behave in unexpected ways when separated from the other genetic material that normally surrounds them. Regulators, modifiers, and essential components may be severed from the genes.

But aside from possibly producing an incomplete or ineffective DNA segment or gene product, an even more dangerous possibility exists of creating new and perhaps harmful variants. The insertion of foreign DNA segments into viral or plasmid DNA is potentially risky. It is possible that new life forms will be produced. It is possible that potent genes might be inadvertently interfered with, perhaps disrupting normal control and regulatory mechanisms. The results of such an interruption are unknown; they could be disastrous. Scientists suspect that cancer is related to a breakdown in control mechanisms and the unleashing of extremely powerful oncogenes (cancer genes), and it is feared that a viral-human DNA combination could exert a similar decontrol effect.

These are not wild fears dreamed up by demagogues who know nothing of genetics. It was exactly issues such as these that the scientists themselves discussed at the Asimolar conference. Work with certain varieties of genes, including the insertion of suspected cancer genes into viral DNA and common bacteria, has been discontinued precisely because of the unknown consequences and potential dangers involved. And it was because of these dangers that safety guidelines were established.

But even safety guidelines are not enough to guarantee that things won't go wrong. Voluntary compliance and effective enforcement are necessary but very difficult to achieve. Past experience has shown that despite existing regulations for the handling of dangerous substances, accidents leading to serious illness and death occur all too often. Sometimes problems stem from faulty equipment, but often the source of trouble is the carelessness of a scientist, or a shortcut taken by a technician. In 1972 at London's School of Tropical Medicine and Hygiene, where the staff has had long experience in dealing with dangerous diseases, an employee contracted smallpox through carelessness. Before the disease had been properly diagnosed, two other persons became infected, and all three died.

In the United States dangerous experiments are often confined to specially equipped laboratory facilities such as those at Fort Detrick, Maryland. Despite sophisticated equipment and safety procedures, there have nonetheless been 425 infections and 3 deaths at Fort Detrick—all of them attributable to dangerous viruses at that facility. In one incident, an employee inadvertently sprayed a laboratory with an aerosol can containing plague virus. At another special safety facility, a laboratory worker contracted a serious virus when a protective glove split and exposed his hand. At Harvard, cockroach infestation in old laboratory buildings posed the problem of spreading infections throughout the community. Such breaches of safety rules and enforcement are always serious, but if they were to involve dangerous newly created living molecules with which medical science had no experience, the results could be catastrophic for the human race.

Still other considerations must be taken into account. No one knows what effect the creation of new forms of life will have on the balance of nature. James D'Annielli, director of the Center for Theoretical Biology at the State University of New York in Buffalo, has predicted that within a few years scientists will have the capacity "to create new species" and "carry out ten billion years of evolution in one year." What are the consequences of humanity's ability to manipulate evolution in such a drastic way? It has taken nature several billion years to perfect the genetic program through evolution, fine-tuning it slowly and gradually, not only maintaining a balance within the genetic program itself, but also establishing an ecological balance between different species of animal and plant life within the environment. The human race has already done much to disrupt this ecological balance, and in recent decades there has been a growing concern about this in society. But the damage done to nature's ecological balance by pollution over the years would pale in significance beside the damage that could be done by the introduction of totally new living organisms into the environment.

The General Electric Company has already used recombinant techniques to create a new type of bacterium that feeds on oil and could be used to clean up oil spills. These bacteria would be released literally to eat up the oil. But the process of releasing such an organism into the environment is fraught with dangers. What impact will this new organism have on fish and plant life in the ocean? What will happen to the bacterium after it consumes the oil? Will it disappear, or will it evolve gradually, and in what direction? How will it affect the balance of nature?

Serious questions have been raised even in cases that don't involve the creation of new forms of DNA, but merely attempt to correct genetic defects. What are the implications of such genetic insertions for normal development of the individual? What impact results from the inexact nature of the genetic material implanted? What possible effects will there be on normal development if fertilization occurs by artificial means? Will there be psychological as well as physical or medical consequences for the individual? No one knows the answers to such questions.

These scientific and technical considerations lead to important political and moral questions. Even before the advent of recombinant DNA, some people voiced fears about the consequences of our increasing ability to make reproductive choices stemming from prenatal diagnosis of birth defects. They fear that society will become increasingly impatient with people who suffer from genetic disease that could have been detected before birth. People might come to believe that such people should never have been born. Compassion and sympathy for the afflicted might disappear.

The issue gets even more complicated when actual manipulation of the genetic program is involved. What proper uses, if any, should society make of this ability? Can human beings be trusted to handle such power in a responsible manner? Who should have the authority to make such decisions?

The track record of humanity in this regard is not very encouraging. Racists and bigots have frequently tried to use theories of genetics for their own purposes, to justify their claims to racial superiority. In the late 1800s, for example, social Darwinists attributed poverty and suffering among the poor to their genetic inheritance rather than to social and economic conditions prevailing in society. Hitler used his misconceptions about genetics to justify the butchery of millions of innocent people. This misuse of genetics is something that many geneticists are very ashamed of and sensitive about; it is something that must not be repeated.

The early statements and predictions about recombinant DNA by many prominent lay persons and scientists seemed to express an almost blind optimism about the benefits of recombinant DNA. For example, a few years ago the prominent scientist Robert L. Sinsheimer said:

> We can begin to confront chance and choice: soon we shall have the power consciously to alter our inheritance, our very nature. . . . The great discoveries in genetics and the great discoveries yet to come open a new dimension of human potential, a new route for the improvement of man. . . . We, mankind, are to have the opportunity to design the future of life, to apply intelligence to evolution. . . . What an outstanding chance and infinite challenge.

Statements like these, which ignore the basic issue of whether it is appropriate for scientists to "alter" humanity's very nature or to "design the future of life," caused many people to worry whether a balanced, judicious approach to this new area of scientific research would be pursued. Dr. Sinsheimer himself eventually took a more balanced view of the potential hazards of recombinant DNA research, moderated his ideas, and came out in favor of certain restrictions on DNA research.

A. M. Chakrabarty, a scientist employed by General Electric, has done research into ways of genetically converting the human digestive tract so that humans could eat cellulose, such as hay and grasses. One problem posed by such a dietary change is the buildup of methane gas in the body. Other researchers talk optimistically about the cosmetic uses of genetic therapy, changing physical traits like hair color, eye color, and height through genetic means. Some postulate the use of genetic modification for mind control. One scientist has been quoted as saying, "Those of us who work in this field see a developing potential for nearly total control of human emotional status, mental functioning, and will to act." Some scientists speculate that genetic treatments one day could be used to alter workers' attitudes of hostility and rebelliousness, of boredom with monotonous tasks, and even to upgrade intellectual levels. It all begins to sound very much like the exercise of totalitarian control in a Brave New World.

Other scientists have made disturbing statements about manipulating the human mind and creating new types of life forms, part human and part animal. For example, scientist Bernard Davis has said, "We cannot exclude the possibility that a few key genes might play an especially large role in determining various intellectual or artistic potentials or emotional patterns." Identification of these key genes, if indeed they do exist, coupled with the techniques of recombinant DNA, would put an incredible degree of power at the disposal of those who would control society. As one scientist put it, geneticists "will correct our mental and social structure." But who would determine what is correct and what is wrong?

J. B. S. Haldane has discussed the possibility of combining life forms, suggesting that in the future astronauts could be genetically altered to resemble monkeys because "a gibbon is better adapted than a man for life in a low gravitational field such as that of a spaceship, an asteroid, or perhaps even the moon. Gene grafting may make it possible to incorporate such features into human stock."

Kimball Atwood of the University of Illinois has suggested the possibility of "an organism that combines the happy qualities of animals and plants, such as one with a large brain so that it can indulge in philosophy and also a photosynthetic area on its back so that it would not have to eat."

Still another area of concern is the potential military use of recombinant DNA research. In the past few years articles have appeared in scientific and military publications speculating about the possible uses of genetic discoveries in warfare. Nobel Laureate Salvador Luria has warned that "we may witness efforts to invent viruses that can spread in an enemy population, genes that produce sensitivity to poisons, or susceptibility to tumors, or even transmissible genetic defects—in other words, genetic genocide." Some military officials and superhawks might find such possibilities tantalizing, but many scientists would question the moral basis of such a distortion of their research, which was motivated by a desire to improve the health and well-being of humanity.

The technological level of recombinant DNA research is still comparatively primitive, and the kinds of manipulation postulated in most of these predictions of the future uses of genetic engineering are still quite distant. But the decision-making process concerning the future of genetic engineering is in motion today, and it is one that must not be left to the scientific experts alone. It concerns the future of life on earth, and it is something that the public must be part of.

The public nature of the debate is particularly important because of the unusually rapid technological progress that has been made in the past few years. Normally there is a time lag of perhaps two or three decades, or even longer, between the theoretical breakthroughs involved in a scientific revolution and the development of the technological capacity to apply theory in practice. But with recombinant DNA, the technological applications have followed rapidly. Previous time lags permitted the further theoretical elaboration in detail, backing up theory with facts, eliminating and anticipating some of the unknowns and potential problems.

But with recombinant DNA the technological applications have followed rapidly, although many unanswered questions remain. The possibility of huge profits to be made has meant the proliferation of private companies, which are not necessarily motivated by concern for the common social welfare.

To get an idea of the rapid growth of this gene-splicing industry, one need only look at the rise of Genetech, one of the four pioneering small companies in the field. Founded in 1976 when two partners invested $500 each and secured $100,000 in seed money to fund research, by 1981 the total capitalization of Genetech had reached $11.3 million. Shares in the firm were worth over $100 million on the stock market. Since 1980 large pharmaceutical and chemical companies including Pfizer, Upjohn, Hoffman-LaRoche, Eli Lilly, Dow, DuPont, Exxon, and General Electric have invested in genetic research. Predictions are that by the end of the 1980s genetic engineering will be a $3 to 5 billion industry.

Researchers are confident that genetic engineering will in a few years' time permit the reliable and inexpensive production of important drugs needed to treat patients. This includes the production of insulin for treating diabetics, and interferon, which is used for treating cancer patients and patients suffering from other diseases caused by unknown sources, presumably viruses. It is anticipated that genetic engineering will permit hemophilia victims to be treated with special factors usually missing from their blood.

Some of the bigger chemical and pharmaceutical companies that have gone into recombinant DNA work have recently been acquiring seed companies and are experimenting with applying the same technology to the genetic manipulation of plants with the goal of producing larger plant crops and plants with cells richer in desired nutrients.

Concerns are raised that the early involvement of private companies motivated by the drive for profits is not conducive to thoughtful decisions on issues with profound social implications. Again, as the experiece of chemical waste dumping and nuclear energy has shown, the track record of private industry in this regard is not very good.

At any rate, the debate that goes on today about recombinant DNA is not simply a technical one; it is ethical, moral, and social as well. It is ultimately a debate about the future of our society. Perhaps Senator Edward Kennedy summed up the issues best in his concluding remarks at the 1976 hearings on genetic engineering, at which he presided:

> ... there is an enormous area of uncertainty surrounding this whole area of recombinant DNA research.
>
> No one can predict with any degree of absolute certainty ... what the dangers would be, or what the opportunities and advantages would be. ... When some of our most

skilled . . . and thoughtful scientists and researchers point out the dangers, they spell out a real living holocaust for this nation . . . and the world, and when they use their minds to elaborate on the possibilities of benefits to mankind, [they show that these benefits] are virtually unlimited. . . .

I think it is absolutely essential that the public be brought into this process. I think if there is a continuing echo from the course of these hearings, it is the importance of the public being informed about this particular issue, understanding the potential hazards and benefits. I believe that they are fully competent to try to sift through the complexities of the potential dangers.

This is a debate that all of us will be involved in during the years ahead.

Glossary

Amino acids   Organic molecules that are the building blocks of protein. Some amino acids are produced within the cell. Others must be obtained from the environment.

Amniocentesis   Extraction of amniotic fluid containing fetal cells, used in prenatal diagnosis.

Carcinogen   Agent that may induce cancer.

Cell   The basic unit of life, a cell is the smallest living thing that can feed, grow, and reproduce independently.

Centromere   Also called a primary constriction, the centromere is the point at which the duplicated parts of a chromosome are joined together.

Chromosome   A chain of genetic material coded in DNA in the cell nucleus. DNA assumes this squat, rodlike chromosome appearance only during cell division. At other times it appears as diffuse threads called chromatin.

Cytogenetics   The science that studies the number and structure of chromosomes.

DNA   Deoxyribonucleic acid, the chemical substance that codes the genetic information.

Embryo   An animal or plant in the early stages of development. In human beings the developing baby is referred to as an embryo until the end of the eighth week of pregnancy.

Enzyme   A protein that can initiate or facilitate a highly specific chemical reaction in the cell.

Fetoscopy   A technique used for visualizing the fetus in prenatal diagnosis.

Fetus   An unborn animal in the later stages of development in the uterus. In human beings the developing baby is referred to as a fetus from the beginning of the ninth week of pregnancy until birth.

Gametes   The reproductive cells (sperms and egg cells) of sexually reproducing organisms containing half of a full complement of the genetic program.

Gene   A segment of the chemical DNA, which carries a basic unit of hereditary information in coded form.

Genetic code   The base triples that specify the twenty different amino acids.

Genetic program   The full set of genetic information coded in DNA. The program governs and controls development and functioning of living organisms.

Genetic screening   Testing a population to identify individuals at risk for a particular genetic disorder or for bearing a child with such a disorder.

Inborn error   A genetically determined biochemical disorder involving an enzyme defect that interferes with the normal metabolic pathway.

Karyotype   The ordered arrangement of all the chromosomes from a single cell.

Meiosis   Cell division that produces reproductive cells carrying only a single representative of each chromosome pair.

Metabolism   The breakdown and buildup of cellular products through chemical reactions in the cell.

Mitosis   Cell division within a living body that produces daughter cells similar to the mother cell, carrying a complete set of genetic material.

Molecule   The smallest unit into which any substance can be divided and still retain its original characteristics.

Mutagen   A substance that induces an inheritable change in the genetic material (mutation).

Mutation   The source of all genetic variation. It is the sudden change in the genetic material of any organism. Its impact may be felt through a change in production of protein.

Recombinant DNA   DNA that is artificially synthesized, involving the insertion of a gene or part of a gene of one organism into the genetic material of another.

RNA   Ribonucleic acid, the general name for three substances that are used to transcribe and translate the genetic code contained in the DNA. The substances are messenger RNA (mRNA), ribosomal RNA (r-RNA), and transfer RNA (tRNA). They all appear as chains modeled after corresponding strands of DNA. Messenger RNA carries the coded genetic message from the cell nucleus to the cytoplasm. Translation of the message carried by mRNA takes place at cell substructures called ribosomes, the major component of which is RNA. Transfer RNA brings amino acids in the sequence specified by the mRNA to the ribosomes in order to produce the proper proteins.

Teratogen   An agent that causes birth defects by disrupting the normal processes of prenatal development.

Bibliography of Sources

Bloom, A., and James, L., eds. *Birth Defects: Original Article Series*, Vol. VII, No. 1. New York: Alan R. Liss, 1981.

Bornstein, Jerry, and Bornstein, Sandy. *What Is Genetics?* New York: Julian Messner, 1979.

Goodfell, June. *Playing God*. New York: Random House, 1977.

Hack, M. S., and Lance, H., eds. *The ACT Cytogenetics Laboratory Manual*. Association of Cytogenetic Technologists, 1980.

Hamerton, J. L. *Human Cytogenetics*. New York: Academic Press, 1971.

Harris, Harry. *The Principles of Human Biochemical Genetics*. New York: Elsevier North-Holland, 1970.

Howard, Ted, and Rifkin, Jeremy. *Who Should Play God?* New York: Dell, 1977.

Hsu, T. C. *Human and Mammalian Cytogenetics: An Historical Perspective*. New York: Springer-Verlag, 1979.

Junis, J. J. *Human Chromosome Methodology*, 2nd ed. New York: Academic Press, 1974.

Karyogram, publication of the Association of Cytogenetic Technologists.

Koller, Peo C. *Recent Results in Cancer Research: The Role of Chromosomes in Cancer Biology*. New York: Springer-Verlag, 1972.

Kruzi, P. F., and Patterson, M. K. *Tissue Culture—Methods and Applications*. New York: Academic Press, 1973.

McAuliffe, Sharon, and McAuliffe, Kathleen. *Life for Sale*. New York: Coward, McCann & Geoghegan, 1981.

Milunsky, Aubrey, ed. *Genetic Disorders and the Fetus: Diagnosis, Prevention, Treatment*. New York: Plenum Press, 1979.

National Foundation, March of Dimes. *An International System for Human Cytogenetic Nomenclature*. Birth Defects: Original Article Series, Vol. XIV, No. 8 (1978).

Paul, John. *Cell and Tissue Culture*, 5th ed. Churchill-Livingstone Press, 1975.

Schulz-Schaeffer, Jurgen. *Cytogenetics*. New York: Springer-Verlag, 1980.

Sutton, H. Eldon, and Harris, Maureen I. *Mutagenic Effects of Environmental Contaminants*. New York: Academic Press, 1972.

Thompson, J., and Thompson, M. *Genetics in Medicine*. Philadelphia: Saunders, 1980.

Index

About the Authors

Sandy Bornstein graduated from Barnard College and holds a master's degree in human genetics from McGill University. She has worked in the medical genetics program at Brookdale Medical Center and is currently supervisor at the New York University–Bellevue Medical Center Cytogenetics Laboratory. Her husband, Jerry, who graduated from New York University, is senior news archives researcher for a television network. He is also a freelance writer who has had a number of articles published in newspapers and magazines. Together the Bornsteins wrote *What Is Genetics?* They live with their two daughters in a renovated brownstone house in New York City.